AF541164

NORTH-EAST INDIA IN INDIA-ASEAN RELATIONS

A STRATEGIC AND DEVELOPMENTAL PERSPECTIVE

NORTH-EAST INDIA
IN
INDIA-ASEAN RELATIONS

A STRATEGIC AND DEVELOPMENTAL PERSPECTIVE

By

Kumar Padmapani Bora, *IRS*

M.A., LLM., M.Phil.

DISCOVERY PUBLISHING HOUSE PVT. LTD.

NEW DELHI-110 002

Published by:
Tilak Wasan

DISCOVERY PUBLISHING HOUSE PVT. LTD.
4383/4B, Ansari Road, Darya Ganj
New Delhi-110 002 (India)
Phone : +91-11-23279245, 43596064-65
Fax : +91-11-23253475
E-mail : discoverypublishinghouse@gmail.com
sales@discoverypublishinggroup.com
parul.wasan@gmail.com
web : www.discoverypublishinggroup.com

***First Edition:* 2014**

ISBN: 978-93-5056-455-4

North-East India in India-ASEAN Relations
A Strategic and Developmental Perspective

© 2014, Author

All rights reserved. No part of this publication should be reproduced, stored in a retrieval system, or transmitted in any form or by any means: electronic, mechanical, photocopying, recording or otherwise, without the prior written permission of the author and the publisher.

This book has been published in good faith that the material provided by authors is original. Every effort is made to ensure accuracy of material, but the publisher and printer will not be held responsible for any inadvertent error(s). In case of any dispute, all legal matters are to be settled under Delhi jurisdiction only.

Printed at:
Dynamic Printers
Delhi

DEDICATED
TO
"*MAA*"

Tarun Gogoi

Chief Minister, Assam
Guwahati

Dispur
6th May, 2013

MESSAGE

I am happy to know that Kumar Padmapani Bora, IRS, is bringing out a book on "North-East India in India-ASEAN Relations: *A Strategic and Developmental Perspective*", soon.

Enhancing relations with ASEAN has been central to India's "Look East Policy" and there has been steady progress in the ASEAN-India relations since the policy was initiated in early 90s.

India's vision of a close relationship with ASEAN is to forge a vast 'arc of prosperity' across Asia. ASEAN region is central to the emerging security and economic architecture in the region. The launch of the Regional Comprehensive Economic Partnership (RCEP) negotiations between ASEAN and its six free-trade partners, including India will culminate in the formation of the largest free trade zone that will bring enormous benefits, peace and prosperity to the peoples of our region.

India and ASEAN economies have withstood the global economic crisis relatively well. Our combined GDP of US$ 3 trillion and population of 1.8 billion with a huge and young workforce constitute a formidable comparative advantage. India-ASEAN bilateral trade has grown, by over 10 times in the last decade, and stands at nearly US$ 80 billion today.

The ASEAN-India Free Trade Agreement in Goods is contributing to the increased trade between India and ASEAN. I am confident that the free trade agreement in services and investment will give a further boost to trade and services and facilitate movement of professionals across the region.

India and ASEAN are poised to create a web of closer rail, road and air links. The dream of the India-Myanmar-Thailand Trilateral Highway is on course to become reality by 2016 and is poised to be extended to Lao and Cambodia. From India's point of view, this will be the highway of prosperity for India's northeastern states by linking them to vibrant markets and high-tech hubs of Southeast Asia.

A new highway project that will connect India, Myanmar, Laos, Vietnam and Cambodia has also been cleared.

Clearly, physical connectivity is not enough. A host of recent initiatives have sought to position people at the heart of this vibrant relationship. The cultural connections were rekindled when the India-ASEAN car rally, that traversed over 8,000 km across the region, brought alive centuries-old civilizational linkages between India and the ASEAN.

Assam shares a strong cultural and linguistic affinity with the ASEAN region in the form of the Tai-Ahom legacy. Historically, Assam has been a melting pot of various racial stocks, namely Indo-Tibeto-Burmese, Mongoloid, Austro Asiatic, Aryan, Dravidian etc. Assam has the unique locational advantage of being situated close to Myanmar, which is the gateway to ASEAN.

South East Asia is one of the fastest growing regions in the world today and enjoys the reputation of being business and investment friendly. Due to its high rate of growth, the ASEAN markets are seeing a massive surge in consumer demand. Assam has the potential to emerge as a strategic base for foreign and domestic investors to tap the vast potential of contiguous markets of Myanmar, China, Malaysia, Thailand, Philippines, Cambodia, Indonesia and other East and South East Asian countries which constitute almost half of the world's population.

Border points at Moreh, Sutarkandi, Mankachar and Dawki have been opened for bilateral trade and commerce. Assam's internal waterways network connects to Bangladesh giving it access to the ports of Chittagong, Kolkata and Haldia. Thus, both the land and water routes are available to investors for re-export to East and South East Asia. Assam's proximity to the SAARC countries of Bangladesh, Nepal and Bhutan would also enable foreign investors to take advantage of the expanding opportunities for regional integration through intra-regional trade under SAARC Preferential Trading Agreement (SAPTA).

There should be direct flights from ASEAN countries to LGB International Airport, Guwahati to increase the possibilities of enhancement in volume of trades, commerce, investment as well as tourism not only in Assam but in the entire North Eastern Region. Moreover, the ASEAN countries, having their consular offices at Kolkata, must extend their visa offices to Guwahati to facilitate greater people-to-people contact as well as trade and commerce.

The intertwining of the destinies of India and the ASEAN, and the larger East Asia is a good news story that is still unfolding. It's a journey that is set to cross new milestones in the future.

It is against this backdrop, I hope Bora's book will throw more light on the emerging prospects of India-ASEAN relationship and also come up with invaluable suggestions as to how to address the problems effectively..

I have no doubt that the book will be well-received by the readers, the foreign policy-makers and the leaders who count a lot.

(TARUN GOGOI)

दून विश्वविद्यालय DOON UNIVERSITY
मोथरोवाला रोड, केदारपुर, पो.ओ. अजबपुर, देहरादून-248001 (उत्तराखण्ड) भारत
Mothrowala Road, Kedarpur, P.O. Ajabpur, Dehradun - 248001 (Uttarakhand) INDIA

Prof. (Dr.) V.K. Jain, *D. Phil. (Sussex U.K.)*
प्रो0 वी. के. जैन
Vice Chancellor / कुलपति

No................................./VC-DU/20

Dated : 12 th May 2013.

MESSAGE

The author presents a very compelling rationale for developing North-East (NE) India as a Gateway to ASEAN countries as part of India's 'Look-East Policy'. Given India's strategic as well as developmental imperatives, it can hardly afford not to engage ASEAN countries for larger objective of peace and stability in the south east Asian region. When large parts of our country and in particular ME states are in dire need of investments for creating requisite infrastructure and resources, it is imperative that the country also makes special efforts to reach out to ASEAN, In this context, the author highlights usefulness of India's cultural, linguistic and ethnic ties with most of ASEAN countries since pre-independence colonial times to the present with specific reference to NE states. The emergence of ASEAN as a significant player in the world economy makes it all the more imperative to develop economic, social and cultural relations with them. The author argues that investments from ASEAN in India and vice-versa would auger well for the development and peace of the region. Towards this end, one of the measures suggested by the author includes opening the borders of NE states with Myanmar to facilitate trade and commerce with ASEAN. Notwithstanding that NE states as Gateway may invite problems of cross-border drug trafficking and terrorism, the author makes a very forceful argument for having NE states as catalysts for a win-win situation both for India and ASEAN for giving impetus to economic growth and development leading to peace and prosperity for their people.

(Prof. V. K. Jain)

An Insight to North-East India in India-ASEAN Relations

Historically India's North East and Burma-Purba Banga (Bangladesh) was a geographical block and practically functioned as a distinct economic zone till the Second World War, India's partition in the aftermath of consolidation of the 'two nation theory' and finally India's attaining Independence in 1947.

Bangladesh and India, today, as two countries share 4,095 km border. Both the countries are members of SAARC and BIMSTEC and signatories of agreements such as SAPTA and SAFTA.

Geography plays a crucial role in shaping the nature and level of economic transaction between these two close neighbours. India surrounds Bangladesh from three sides. The North-Eastern States of India (NESI) have a large share in this geographical adjacency, with four out of the seven sharing border with Bangladesh: Assam, Meghalaya, Mizoram, and Tripura.

The mainland India is connected with the North-Eastern States through the narrow Siliguri Corridor, otherwise known as the Chicken's Neck. The seven North-Eastern states have remarkable diversity in their heritage, and yet geographical proximity and parallel economic conditions bind their fates together. The landlocked states have suboptimal land-based trade with the rest of India due to connectivity gap. Despite immense geographical and economic scope, their trade with Bangladesh and other neighbors also remains poor.

Infrastructure and physical capital remain underdeveloped in the sub-region and the populations in most of the states are predominantly rural with share of industrial sector in the Gross State Domestic Product (GSDP) stagnant. In fact, central transfer constitutes a large part of the GSDP of these states, underscoring their underdeveloped economy.

Apart from geographical contiguity, North East and Bangladesh exhibit complementary economic characteristics as well. Before 1947, the erstwhile East Bengal (now Bangladesh) economy was closely aligned with economic activities in Assam, Tripura and other areas that now constitute NER through trade and infrastructural connectivity. The tie was severed with partition. Nonetheless, Bangladesh and the North-Eastern states of India constitute together a veritable economic sub-region, whose developmental synergies continue to remain largely untapped.

With substantial natural resources and investment potential, the NER need to integrate economically not only with the rest of India for their own benefit as well as for India as a whole. One of the important elements to explore this potential to the advantage of all the geographically proximate constituents- such as Bangladesh, Myanmar, Bhutan, NER and the rest of India is to find ways and means that would make transit-based connectivity through Bangladesh and Myanmar, a viable and economically attractive to all these constituents. This may also open up horizons for Bangladesh, and India to reach out to the vibrant ASEAN economies, including Myanmar which is coming out of its shell and being recognized as in important economic hub and trade partner for this region. The landlocked countries can enhance their trade logistics with better access to the geographically proximate Chittagong port. The benefits from such access for the Indian economy will be vast.

Like Bangladesh, our immediate neighbor Myanmar is of strategic and economic importance for India. These two nations share a 1,600 km land border and a long maritime boundary in the strategically important Bay of Bengal and

Andaman Sea. Both nations are bound by historical, religious, cultural and ethnic linkages. As the land of Lord Buddha, India is a country of pilgrimage for the people of Myanmar. Four of India's politically-sensitive Northeastern states share international borders with Myanmar. Ethnic populations of these states have been divided by artificial borders drawn up by the British at the time of Myanmar's independence and subsequently, consequent to the Indian Government giving Myanmar the Chindwin Valley. Consequently, both nations face insurgency by some of these groups in border regions. As a result, the border regions of both countries are under developed. Frequent disruptions in trade and other activities are also a result.

It was at this stage that India also announced it's 'Look East Policy'-primarily directed at improving the situation in India's North East through close ties and projects through Myanmar and South East Asia. Unfortunately, little has been done since to fulfill the policy's primary aim and the border region's problems remain inadequately addressed through badly planned and executed projects in Myanmar such that they have lost a great deal of confidence in us.

India needs to develop the Northeast region so that it can be used as the hub for export to Myanmar and beyond. For this, Special Economic Zones need to be set up in the region. These would promote the establishment of consumer, engineering, and food-processing industries. Infrastructure in the Northeast needs to be improved on an urgent basis. For this, various Ministries of the Government of India should work in tandem with the State Governments of the region.

Alternative routes to Myanmar should be opened through Manipur via Silchar connecting Moreh. Other routes can be opened via Avakhung Pansat in the Somra Hills in Nagaland. In Mizoram, Aizawl-Champhai-Zowkathar and Rhi route can be built and subsequently extended to Parwa via the Kaladan-Sittwe route. Route through Udaipur in Tripura can also be explored rather than connecting Indian and China through the Stilwell road.

The Chapters of this book have dealt with the significant issues involved in making North-East India as a gateway to ASEAN and with a positive note I hope that this book will surely help in the areas of research, policy making and investment purpose in the near future.

Sri Pradyut Bordoloi

Minister of Industry & Commerce, Power

Government of Assam

Foreword

In recent years India's North-East has emerged as a priority area in enhancing closer relations with ASEAN. In previous years, India was riveted by serious threats to its security from armed attacks by anti Indian insurgents operating in India's North-East, an area which in public imagination was remote both culturally and ethnically.

India's shares 1643 km with Myanmar through its North-East states, did not foster links which had existed between North East and the contiguous region in pre-colonial and colonial period. Thus, before 1990s' there was no desire on India's part to build connectivity with Myanmar which was mired by its own domestic problems with serious ethnic insurgency of its own. In 1992, the overthrow of a democratic government in Myanmar by the army under General Ne Win, added a new troublesome neighbour to India's already irksome neighbourhood. North-East's connectivity with Myanmar in terms of culture, ethnicity and geography was not seen as an asset but rather a liability where insurgents found sympathisers among the ethnic groups across the border that was equally keen to succeed from Myanmar.

During the Cold War era, India's foreign policy towards Southeast Asia in general and ASEAN in particular was marked by slow progress and static policies, rather than change and dynamism. Inspite of close historical, cultural and geographical links with Southeast Asia, India's foreign policy towards Southeast Asia was an indication of its own participation in the whirlpool of Cold War politics, besides, it could not detach itself from its preoccupation with its own strategic problems. The 1962 war inflicted by China and wars with Pakistan occupied much of India's had strategic implications on India's foreign policy. Myanmar's growing closeness to China and latter's supply of arms to insurgents in North-East was viewed by India as a major threat to its territorial integrity.

A paradigm shift in India's policy towards ASEAN took shape in the 90's. The end of the Cold War coincided with a Congress government headed by Narsimha Rao coming to power in India in 1991. Rao initiated the Look East Policy and introduced key reforms in order to liberalise the Indian economy. With these policies in place there was now a firm basis for cooperation between India and ASEAN. It laid down the conceptual framework of India's policy in engaging Southeast Asian countries both bilaterally and multiletrally. Early years of Look East Policy, North-East figured as more of a concern due to its insurgency problem, than as an asset in being a gateway to Southeast Asia. Visualising Northeast as India's gateway to Southeast Asia is unthinkable without the cooperation of Myanmar. China's emergence as a major influence in Yangon had grown to such an extent that it alarmed India and ASEAN countries of its serious strategic consequences. India realised that by not engaging with the military regime India was being marginalised which was not a pragmatic approach. The Look East policy now include building relations with Myanmar with positive response from its regime resulting in close economic ties; with Myanmar's inclusion in ASEAN the interaction is no longer confined to bilateral meetings. The mutual desire to engage each other has helped in joint military operations against insurgency in India's North-East as well against drug trafficking and illegal immigrants. Good relations with Myanmar has also led to India getting access to its rich energy-producing resources-critical to India's growing needs.

There are challenges as there are prospects for a better future for the states of North East. Political will is essential to carry out the implementation of road and rail networks between North-East and the ASEAN states for successful economic development and integration. In the not so distant past it would have been unconcealed to envisage that the ASEAN- India Car rally starting from Guwahati would become a reality. A trilateral highway to link India through Northeast with Myanmar and Thailand is being imitated. The highly ambitious proposal to connect Guwahati with Asian Highway which will connect "India from Mandalay in Myanmar via Moreh in Manipur and pass through Nagaland before entering Assam through Golaghat district." Though the land connectivity between ASEAN and India has a long way to go, these events do generate a feeling of déjà vu.[1] Today, after decades of military rule, there is a transition towards democracy in Myanmar. President Thein Sein has promised several reforms in the political and economic sectors. Assumption is, If right policies are pursued by the so called "civilian government" then Myanmar could "emerge as the richest country on mainland of Southeast Asia" (Steinberg). Despite the changes, which saw release of Aung San Suu Kyi from house arrest and her winning a by-election for a parliamentary seat, recent days have been marred by communal violence in Myanmar's Rakhine State, bringing out the predicament of the Muslim Rohingyas. Despite some setbacks, it is generally held that a genuine political reconciliation is definitely taking place after years of armed ethnic conflict. Peace agreement was signed with almost all ethnic groups. The change in the political scenario is seeing a flow of foreign investors and businessmen in Myanmar; although without proper guidelines it could lead to mercenary exploitation of resources and finally to turmoil with serious consequences for bordering country like India. Peace and stability in Myanmar is critical to India's security, besides peace and stability in Myanmar it will lead to greater economic engagement with benefits accruing to marginalised states of North-East.

1 Www.aseansec.org\16594.htm-37k

Padmapani Bora has written an insightful book on India's focus in building partnership through North-East with Southeast Asia. He has presented in great detail the concept of Northeast India as a gateway to Southeast Asian region. He has examined the paradigm shift in India's foreign policy in the post cold era through the initiative of Look East policy. Padmapani Bora belongs to the North-East, besides he has studied and researched on the issue at the School of International Studies, JNU, New Delhi and is currently serving as Assistant Commissioner Income Tax at Government of India. He brings a fresh perspective to the efforts being made by India for a meaningful economic integration of the North-East with the ASEAN. Padmapani has explained the challenges that have to be overcome if India's North-East has to emerge as a major component of the Look East policy. This book in my view should prove to be invaluable to policy makers, scholars and students.

Prof. Manmohini Kaul

Centre for South, Central, South East Asian and South West pacific Studies

School of International Studies

Jawaharlal Nehru University

New Delhi-110067, INDIA

Preface

In the post Cold War period India and ASEAN countries have revived their economic relations which were badly affected during the Cold War. Continuous interest in each other in the changed world order has strengthened the relationship. India in the early 90s initiated the "Look East Policy" with a view of closer engagement with its extended neighbourhood in the East. The engagement so far has led to cooperation in many fields, from economic to defence – strategic. India's inclusion as full dialogue partner of ASEAN in 1995, membership in ASEAN Regional Forum (ARF) in 1996, its inclusion in the East Asia Summit (EAS) in December 2005 and recent India-ASEAN FTA have been a part of a continuing process of mutual engagement. Both India and ASEAN has showed interest to have Summit level diplomacy and a new direction was started with the first ASEAN-India Summit, held in Phnom Penh in the year 2002. India's entry to ADSEAN Treaty of Amity and Cooperation (TAG) in 2003 has further contributed to greater engagement.

There has been much talk that North-East can emerge as a gateway to ASEAN region. This eastern most region of India shares a long international boundary with Myanmar. Considering the significance of the region, first ASEAN-India car rally on 23 November, 2004 was flagged off in Guwahati by Prime Minister Dr. Manmohan Singh. Various steps have already been taken to liberalize trade via North-East India. Although it is considered as welcome step, some scholars have highlighted possible security treat and other apprehensions in the whole process.

This book deals with the strategic and developmental issues of India-ASEAN relations with special emphasis on India's North-East Region. Central idea is to bring North-East India into the pivot to understand India-ASEAN Relations and accordingly direct future policy initiatives. It is divided into five chapters.

The first chapter is an introductory one. Chapter gives an idea about the historical understanding of India ASEAN relationship in the pre-colonial era in terms of religion, language, culture and civilization along with colonial period when India became more closer to Southeast Asian region with the ground formation of Indian National Army led by Netaji Subhash Chandra Bose in the soil of Southeast Asia followed by the post-colonial developments since the special conference on Indonesia that was held in January 1949 attended by 15 nations including India expressing support to Sukarno led armed struggle against Dutch colonial rule. The chapter discusses the background of formation of ASEAN and its current developments including ASEAN +3 and ASEAN +1. The chapter has also discussed the evolvement of the diplomacy of Look East Policy in length and its current developments. Discussions have been made on the recent development on Indo-ASEAN relationship in terms of strategic importance, trade including Free Trade Agreements (FTA) and bilateral relationships. Lastly, an idea has been given on Northeast India in the framework of Look East Policy.

In the second chapter geo-political importance of Northeast India, its strategic location viz-a-vis to ASEAN region have been discussed. The study covers traditional and cultural connectivity of Northeast India with Southeast Asian countries in historical perspectives. In this chapter discussions have been made on demographic profile of the region along with the geo-politics of Northeast India. It also discusses the historical connectivity in terms of language and ethnicity.

The third chapter focuses on border connectivity between New Delhi and ASEAN bloc via Northeastern region and the different initiatives that have been taken in this connection.

Discussions have been made on the Indo-ASEAN car rally, the economic prospects from opening of 'Stilwell Road' with latest developments along with China factor, 'Kaladan Multi Model' transport project which will connect India with Myanmar-particularly India's Northeastern States, 'Asian Highway Project' which will provide further basis for co-operation among BIMST-EC. The chapter also highlights the security and related cross-border issues.

The forth chapter draws attention to the economic aspect. The Northeast India has immense potential. Efforts must be directed to tap its resources to give fillip to trade with its neighborhood. The chapter discusses on economic developments that may come to Northeast India as a part of Look as East Policy. Prospective areas of tourism, power sector, indigenous industries and export prospects from Northeast India to ASEAN countries have been looked at. Border trade with Myanmar and its potentials have been discussed in details. Focus is also being laid on peace and good governance which are termed as keys to development in the region.

The concluding chapter sums up the finding of the study. This chapter also seeks to evaluate future prospects of the initiative of making North-East as a gateway to ASEAN region. Chapters talks about how to extract the best potentials of geo-politics and ethnic commonality of the North-East India with the ASEAN Region.

—Author

Acknowledgements

I was assisted by several individuals whose suggestions and advises have been of significant value. I would like to thank a few people for their support and guidance in bringing this book forward from the confines of my study room.

At the onset I would like to extend my gratitude to Professor Manmohini Kaul from Jawaharlal Nehru University, New Delhi. As a guide and mentor professor Kaul's insightful views have contributed immensely in the research process of the book.

I would also like to thank Professor Ganganath Jha from Jawaharlal Nehru University, New Delhi for his valuable advise.

I would like extend my heartfelt gratitude to my beloved father Prabin Kumar Bora without whose love and support these accomplishments wouldn't have been ever possible.

I especially extent my thanks to my wife Mridusmita for her all-time encouragement in bringing out this book.

I am highly grateful to Tilak Wasan and his Discovery Publishing House Pvt. Ltd. for coming forward to publish my work.

Last, but of course not the least, I would also thank all the individuals specially J.K. Manocha, who in some ways have helped me in this journey.

13 May, 2013 **Kumar Padmapani Bora**

Contents

Abbreviations

ANLA : Adivasi National liberation Association
APEC : Asia-Pacific Economic Cooperation
ASEAN : Association of South East Asian Nation
ARF : ASEAN Regional Forum
BIMSTEC : Bay of Bengal Initiative for Multi-Sectored Technical and Economic Cooperation
CECA : Comprehensive Economic Cooperation Agreement
CII : Confederation of Indian Industries
DHD : Dima Halong Deoga
DoNER : Development of North Eastern Region
EAS : East Asian Summit
EPZ : Export Processing Zone
ENRC : Eastern Naga Regional Council
ESCAP : Economic and Social Commission for Asia and the Pacific
FTA : Free Trade Agreement
FDI : Foreign Direct Investment
GDP : Gross Domestic Product
INA : Indian National Army
ICC : Indian Chamber of Commerce
ICMR : Indian Council for Medical Research
KIA : Kachin Independence Army

KLNLF	:	Karbi-Longri National Liberation Front
KLO	:	Karbi Liberation Organization
MGC	:	Mekong-Ganga Cooperation
MNF	:	Manipuri National Front
NACO	:	National Aids Control Organization
NATO	:	North Atlantic Treaty Organization
NDFB	:	National Democratic Front of Bodoland
NEEPCO	:	North Eastern Electric Power Cooperation Limited
NNC	:	Naga Nationalist Council
NSCN	:	National Socialist Council of Nagaland
RITES	:	Rail India Technical Economic Services
SEATO	:	South-East Asian Treaty Organization
SAARC	:	South Asian Association for Regional Cooperation
TAC	:	Treaty of Amity and Cooperation
ULFA	:	United Liberation Front of Assam
UPA	:	United Progressive Alliance

1

Introduction

Foreign policy and diplomacy act as the steering wheel of international relations. No state can live in isolation. Every state seeks to promote its own interests. Foreign policy is formulated by every state to maximize its national interests. It is concerned with both change and *status quo.* Its formulation is a dynamic process, influenced by different factors. Geographical factor is a basic determinant. Likewise history, tradition, possession of raw materials and natural resources, political organization, tradition, forms of government, enlightened leadership all contribute a lot to the shaping foreign policy (Kappen, 1991). Any change in the international order at any given point of time has direct impact on the foreign policy formulation. One of the major Foreign Policy initiatives that India has adopted in the post Cold War period is its 'Look-East policy'. The "Look-East" policy was launched in 1992 just after the end of the cold war, following the collapse of the Soviet Union. After the start of liberalization, it was formulated as a strategic policy decision taken by the government of India. The motive behind this policy initiative was to have economic, political and strategic engagement with its eastern neighbourhood of Southeast Asia and with ASEAN the crucial regional grouping (Devare, 2006). During the 80s and early 90s the ASEAN economy was recognized world over as booming. Although India has had an age old trade and cultural ties with the region it was due to the Cold War that these ties could not culminate into deeper economic relations. The Look-East policy was an attempt to revive relations with a view of building economic linkages beneficial to both the sides. Since 1992, both India and ASEAN have cooperated in various fields. This initiative also brought about enormous opportunities for bilateral cooperation with the individual countries of Southeast Asia along with sub-regional cooperation like Bay of Bengal Initiative for Multi-Sectored Trade and Economic Cooperation (BIMSTEC) and Mekong Ganga Cooperation (MGC).

The Look East policy is stated to be important also for transforming India's North-Eastern region that shares 1643 Km long border with Myanmar (Sanjib Baruah, 2004). Significantly, the region has cultural and traditional commonality with mainland Southeast Asia and have the potential to connect ASEAN region with India. In this foreign policy context North-East India is described as the gateway to ASEAN. The Look-East policy has emerged as an important factor in promoting economic ties of the North-Eastern states with its neighbour.

Historical Understanding of India-ASEAN Relations

India's association with ASEAN region can be traced back to ancient time. No other country has influenced this region as much as India by way of religion, language, culture and civilization. There is enormous historical evidence to suggest that there were flourishing economic and cultural relations between India and the countries of Southeast Asia in the pre-colonial era. Much commonality is seen in many of the Southeast Asian languages. Temples of Cambodia recall the historical ties with India. Islam, too, travelled via India to Southeast Asia while Buddhism moved from India earlier on (Sarkar, 1985). Similarly, Southeast Asia's cultural impact can be found in India's North-East. During India's freedom struggle different kind of connectivities were also established. Netaji Subhash Chandra Bose formed the India National Army

(INA) on the soil of Southeast Asia. Indian nationalist leaders convened the Asian Relations Conference in New Delhi in March 1947 primarily to express solidarity with the freedom struggles all across Southeast Asia. Equally important was the Special Conference on Indonesia that was held in January 1949 in New Delhi to express support to the Sukarno-led armed struggle against the Dutch colonial rule. In fact, it has been argued that freedom struggles, especially in Indonesia and Vietnam, provided major inputs in shaping the nascent Indian Foreign Policy in the late 1940's. At Bandung Conference of 1955, India played a crucial role in formation of non-aligned Movement (Prakash, et.al, 1996)

ASEAN was formed in 1967 as an ideological counter forum against communism by the leaders of the five major powers in the region, namely Malaysia, Singapore, Indonesia, Thailand and Philippines (Acharya, 2000). The leaders of these countries met in Thailand and signed the ASEAN Declaration, most commonly known as Bangkok Declaration on 8th August 1967(ASEAN Secretariat, 1995). Despite the differences, these countries agreed on common objective to accelerate economic growth, social progress and cultural development in the region and to promote regional peace and stability through abiding respect for justice and rule of law and adherence to the principles of the United Nations Charter. In the recent past ASEAN has emerged one of the most successful regional groupings in both strategic and economic terms despite the economic crisis of 1997-98 (Reddy, 2005).

Today ASEAN comprises of all the ten member countries of the Southeast Asia Indonesia, Malaysia, Thailand, Singapore, the Philippines, Vietnam, Laos, Cambodia, Brunei and Myanmar. Besides having Dialogue Partners, ASEAN has formed new mechanism in the aftermath of financial crisis known as ASEAN +3 (China, South Korea and Japan) and due to growing linkages with India ASEAN +1 in 2002. ASEAN's evolution started only in 1976 with its first ever Summit Meeting at Bali. One of the major policy initiatives taken at this Summit was the signing of the Treaty of Amity and Cooperation (TAC) on 24th February 1976. It declared that in their relations with one another the contracting parties should be guided by certain fundamental principles such as mutual respect, sovereignty, equality, integrity and national interests. This was the most important development since the establishment of ASEAN (Ghosal, 1998.) Today, ASEAN has grown into a large structure with many levels of decision-making from Heads of State or Government to technical groupings. Discussions and decision-making are in the form of formal and informal meetings at each of these levels and Summits at the level of Heads of State which is the highest decision is making body ASEAN. The ASEAN Secretariat in Jakarta was created to act as administrative and operational organ of ASEAN. There are four divisions in the ASEAN structure. These are: Functional Cooperation, Political and Security Cooperation, Economic Cooperation and External Relations. Over the growing concern about the security issues led ASEAN to have an initiative to form ASEAN Regional Forum (ARF) in 1996 (Singh, 1999). The Financial crisis of 1997 placed a question mark on ASEAN's capabilities as a successful regional organization. This period and the years that followed became a watershed in the ASEAN history. The crisis raised doubts about the ability of ASEAN to manage the economic and political challenges that emerged (Mely Callallero-A, 2005). Besides, ASEAN has failed to address the question of Myanmar which had been under military junta for long time. However, in spite of these shortcomings, ASEAN has recovered from the fallout of economic crisis and is successfully leading towards regional integration as stated ASEAN Vision 2020. The ASEAN Vision 2020 affirmed an outward-looking ASEAN playing a pivotal role in the international community and advancing ASEAN's common interests (ASEAN Vision 2020).

In 1949, the Philippines, one of the main pro-U.S countries in the region proposed under the leadership of Foreign Secretary Carlos Rumulo an 'Asiatic Organization' at the conference on Indonesia held in New Delhi in January 1949.

It left a significant impression on the participants and opened the way for future policy initiatives. Quirino, the then President of the Philippines, talked about a Pacific Union in 1947, in his speech before the US Senate. But his conception of this regional grouping was more 'Asiatic' or in other word he wanted to have a cohesive stand among the Asian countries in order to put a barrier in the way of spreading communism in the region. He wrote to General Romulo that:

> *"I have summoned you home to help prepare the necessary groundwork for the prosecution of an important phase of our foreign policy which I consider a timely contribution to the peace of the world: the problem of forging a closer union among the people of South-East Asia dedicated to the maintenance of peace and freedom in the region through appropriate methods of political., economic and cultural cooperation with one another."* (Kaul, 2001)

Quirino planned a conference on 20th May, 1950 to form a non-communist bloc. India, Australia, Sri Lanka, Indonesia, Pakistan, and Thailand were the participating countries. It was an attempt to bring the non-aligned countries together. But the conference could not bring any organizational framework due to the difference of opinion among the participating countries and due to the Philippines close defense and political ties with the United State. Non-aligned countries like India and Indonesia were extremely suspicious of the Philippines proposal.

The spread of communism in Indo-China alarmed the US policy makers and they sponsored the Southeast Asian Treaty Organization (SEATO) which was formed in 1954 (Smith, 1990). It was seen as a preventative measure to control the effect of communist 'domino theory'. It had only two ASEAN countries as members, namely the Philippines and Thailand. The whole idea of SEATO was seen by the non-aligned countries as an attempt by the US to interfere in the internal affairs of Asian countries and an extension of NATO. A parallel development was made by the non-aligned countries. In this regard India, under the leadership of

Jawaharlal Nehru and Indonesia under Sukarno played pivotal role on behalf of Asian-African countries. A conference of Asian-African countries was convened at Bandung in 1955.Although the Philippine was invited, it was considered as a proponent of US policies in Southeast Asia (Acharya, 2000).

In 1959, Malaysian President Tunuku Abdur Rahman showed keenness for a regional organization of the Southeast Asian countries. His initiative had positive impact which led to the formation of Association of South-East Asia (ASA) in July 1961 with three ASEAN countries, Malaysia, the Philippines and Thailand as its core members. Other Southeast Asian countries did not show any interest and many were apprehensive of vis-à-vis its creation. Indonesia found this idea as an attempt to bring non- SEATO countries closer to the U.S led western bloc. Besides its confrontation on political level with Malaysia kept Indonesia away from this regional grouping. Despite such apprehension ASA did succeed in laying the foundation for future cooperation after the fall of Sukarno in 1965.

By 1967, there was improvement in the Indonesia-Malaysia relationship due to change in the political authority with Suharto as the head in Indonesia, and between the Philippines and Malaysia (there were claims by the Philippines over Sabha). With the establishment of ASEAN on the 8th August 1967, five out of ten countries of Southeast Asia, namely the Philippines, Malaysia, Indonesia, Singapore and Thailand, became its core members.

As stated earlier, India's interaction with ASEAN in the Cold War era was limited due to India's suspicion of alliance politics. In the Cold War days most of the then ASEAN countries perceived India to be in the camp of the Soviet Union. India' close ties with the Soviet Union created some amount of distance from anti-communist ASEAN bloc. However India did have bilateral relations with various countries of Southeast Asia then with ASEAN as a regional grouping. India signed a trade accord with Indonesia in 1966, and another such first accord was signed with the Philippines in1968. Bilateral relation with Malaysia witnessed in July 1968 included a vast area of exchange from agriculture to cultural affairs. India did show interest in the affairs of Southeast Asia, and played a major role in the Bandung Conference of 1955. However, the security compulsions on its borders due to China and Pakistan put a damper on India's engagement with Southeast Asia. Also, India's relation with Indonesia detoriated due to latter's support Pakistan during the Indo-Pak war of 1965. When ASEAN was formed in 1967, though India was invited to become a member, it refused to do. India took this stand as New Delhi believed that ASEAN was a pro-West security organization and India tried as much as possible to keep itself non-aligned (Matto, 2001).

By 1976, India's perceptions of ASEAN changed and it requested for the formal Dialogue Partner status. India's Foreign Minister visited ASEAN region in 1976 and a number of joint ventures were finalized with countries like Malaysia, Singapore, and Thailand. In 1977, the first ever non-Congress government at the centre made an attempt to improve India's relations with the ASEAN. It resulted in reciprocal visit of the leaders of ASEAN member countries. But India- AEEAN relation once again got a set beck due to the Vietnamese invasion of Kampuchea in 1978. India's reorganization of the Heng Samrin regime in Kampuchea was not appreciated by ASEAN. Although India refused, AEAN countries thought that India was lobbing for Vietnam and its occupation in Kampuchea which ASEAN refused to recognize (Kaul, 2003).

Indira Gandhi as a Prime Minister in 1981 once again tried to boost India-ASEAN relations. She visited the Philippines and Indonesia. P.V. Narasimha Rao, then Foreign Minister of India visited Malaysia in the same year. These visits showed India's willingness to strengthen its ties with ASEAN which by then had emerged as the hub for economic growth.

During Rajiv Gandhi as the Prime Minister of India, not much could have been done to strengthen the relations with Southeast Asia. It was because of the reason that India, during mid- 80s was trying to have a cohesion within the South Asia and played a leading role in the formation of the South Asian Association of Regional Cooperation (SAARC). New Delhi's foreign policy initiatives were also directed by the ethnic problem in Sri Lanka and problems with Pakistan over Kashmir (Sridharan, 1996).

Thus India's relations with ASEAN before 1990s were mainly directed by the Cold-War politics and the change in India's Foreign Policy towards Southeast Asia was an outcome of the significant changes in the world's political and economic scenario after the end of the Cold-War and India's own march towards economic liberalization (Reddy, 2005). India's search for economic space resulted in our *'Look-east'* policy. This was the first time that India stated approaching ASEAN with a constructive policy framework. ASEAN's potential to become a major partner of India in trade and investment has a significant factor in the policy paradigm. India's policy initiatives had positive response from ASEAN and it offered India a Sectored Membership in 1992 and full Dialogue Partner status in 1995 (Naidu, 1998). Since 1996, India has been an active participant in ARF (Singh, 1999). Over the past decade India has strengthened its ties with ASEAN as well as with the individual members of the region through bilateral diplomatic and economic initiatives like the Free Trade agreement (FTA) with Thailand and Comprehensive Economic Cooperation Agreement (CECA) with Singapore. In return India also attracted FDI from Malaysia, Thailand and Singapore. India's strategic role was finally acknowledged through ASEAN+ One in 2002. One of the major landmarks in Indo-ASEAN relation was the signing of TAC by India in 2003 which ultimately led India to make its entry into the greater East-Asian Community and to attend the East-Asian Summit. Number of new areas of cooperation has emerged such as energy security, combat terrorism, Free Trade agreement, and strategic diplomacy etc.

The Diplomacy of Look-East Policy

India's strong desire to forge a mutually beneficial partnership with the members of the Association of Southeast Asian Nation (ASEAN) led to its "Look-East" policy (Mohan, 2003). According to P.V Narasimha Rao, the then Prime Minister of India, *"The 'Look-East' policy was not mere an external economic policy, it was also a strategic shift in India's vision of the world and India's place in the evolving global economy. Most of all it was about reaching out our civilizational Asian neighbors in the region who, by emerging as regional economic powerhouses, also presented us with a model worthy of emulation"*(Nanda, 2004).

The formulation of 'Look-East' policy had political, economic and strategic considerations. Earlier India's foreign policy was mostly directed by the Pakistan factor, domestic politics and its oil dependence on the Gulf region. Oil dependence on Gulf made it look more to its west then to the east. The political change in the international scene in the late 80s and the Gulf War of early 90s had motivated India's foreign policy makers to give new shape and direction to nation's foreign policy in tune with the changing world politics.

The Balance of Payment crisis in 1991 pushed the government of India to embark on a programme of structural adjustment and economic reform. India made a paradigm shift in its economy by opening it for global market. Indian diplomacy began to promote its potentials abroad, especially in capital surplus economies. Southeast Asia was seen as one of the fastest growing region in the world and, consequently, as a source of Foreign Direct Investment (FDI). It soon became a model of economic growth for Indian economy (Grare and Matto, 2003). Indian government went on to have cooperation with the region in some prime sectors of development such as infrastructure, telecommunication energy etc. The policy of 'Look-East' also was a result of India's exclusion forms the major regional trade groupings due its protectionist economy till the beginning of the process of liberalization. China's inroads into Southeast Asia were a wake up call for Indian policy makers. Some of the ASEAN countries were also keen to have India to play a proactive role and in a way balance the growing economic role of China in the Southeast Asia. They thought that regionalism needed greater integration with East Asia and with countries like India. Besides, if the US could play a role in Asia through APEC, Indian policy makers felt that they had every reason to be part of regional integration taking place in the neibourhood (Shri Prakash, 2004).

Selth (1996) argues that the strategic and border related issues also played an important role in the 'Look-East' initiative. India shares a long border with the Southeast Asian region, mainly with Myanmar. Due to presence of different Indian terrorist outfits in Myanmar and its increased closeness with China made India look for closer ties with its eastern neighbourhood. Presence of huge gas reserves in Myanmar were an added impetus. The peninsular India and Andaman and Nicobar are close to Malaysia, Singapore and Indonesia. Maritime security can be ensured only through coordinated efforts.

Due to the 'Look-East' policy, India's trade with the ASEAN countries has increased from $2.4 billion in 1994 to $23billion in 2005. In political sphere India's relation has been elevated to the summit level which made it easy for India to enter. It is anticipated that it would to India's inclusion in the APEC.

To further build and strengthen ties with ASEAN and to reinforce the 'Look-East' policy, sub-regional groupings like BIMSTEC and MGC have been launched (Kaul, 2006). BIST-EC comprising of Bangladesh, India, Sri Lanka, and Thailand was established in 1997. With Myanmar, and in 2004, Bhutan and Nepal, the grouping came to be known as BIMSTEC or the Bay of Bengal Initiative for Multi-Sectored Technical and Economic Cooperation. The formation of BIMSTEC provides for a union of South and Southeast Asia with the potential of integrating more than 1.3 billion people. An important agenda of the BIMSTEC has been regional cooperation, which would take the form of joint marketing and coordination (Devi, 2007). It has six areas of cooperation: trade and investment, technology, transport and communication, energy, tourism, and fisheries. A framework agreement with the aim of establishing a Free Trade Area (FTA) has also been signed (Sen, et al, 2004)

The other such initiative of MGC includes India, Myanmar, Thailand, Laos, Cambodia, and Vietnam as members. The project is aimed at the development of overland trade, tourism, communication, and transport linkages. The MGC provides a framework for closer cultural and people-to-people links between the people who have historical connectivity. The 'Look-East' strategy has not only led India to strengthen its ties with Southeast Asia and beyond but also to integrate ASEAN region with South Asia through the sub-regional initiative (www.manipuronline.com).

Recent Developments in India-ASEAN Relations

The India-ASEAN relations in the recent past can be analyzed both in political and economic terms. We have already mentioned about the India's engagement with the ASEAN started in the post Cold War period with its sectored membership in 1992. They became firm with the granting of full Dialogue Partner status in 1995 and with India's inclusion in the ARF (Khanna, 2000). The relationship was further concretized with India's elevation to summit level partnership in 2002 at the first India- ASEAN summit held in Phnom Penh on 5 November 2002. This was followed by the India-ASEAN Investment Summit held in India in December, 2002. The first ASEAN-India Summit was the culmination of India's sustained effort to upgrade the Dialogue Partnership with ASEAN. At the Summit, India called for an ASEAN-India FTA within a 10-year time frame (Ariff and Cheen, 2006). The 2nd ASEAN-India Summit held in Bali on 8th October 2003, was a significant landmark in India-ASEAN relations. Major agreements signed here were The Framework Agreement for

Comprehensive Economic Cooperation signed by leaders of the ASEAN and India. Minister of External Affairs of India signed the document of the TAC and also the Joint Declaration on Cooperation in Combating International Terrorism. The accession to the TAC proved to be a major plus point for India in its entry into the East Asia Summit. The East Asian Summit (EAS)—which included China, India, Japan, South Korea, Australia and New Zealand, and the ten ASEAN countries is the first step towards building an East Asian Community. The 3rd India-ASEAN Summit in Vientiane on 29- 30 November, 2004 many significant agreements were signed on "India-ASEAN Partnership for Peace, Progress and Shared Prosperity". The 4th and 5th India-ASEAN Summits were held in Kuala Lumpur and Singapore respectively. In the Singapore Summit held in 2007, the main area of talk was to finalize the Free Trade Agreement between India and ASEAN (Asean Summit, 2007).

Both India and ASEAN's sustained efforts to have cooperation has shown commensurate results. There is still to further expand these ties (Asher, et.al., 2003). At the 2nd India-ASEAN Business Summit held in New Delhi and Mumbai in 2003, a target of US$ 15 billion by 2005 and US$ 30 billion for India ASEAN trade by 2007 was laid out. The target of US$ 30 billion was reiterated by Prime Minister Dr. Manmohan Singh at the 3rd ASEAN-India Summit held in Vientiane on 30th November, 2004. India's exports to ASEAN member countries include oil meals, gems and jewellery, meat and meat preparations, cotton yarn, fabrics, machinery, rice, drugs and pharmaceuticals, chemicals, etc. Our imports mainly consist of artificial resins, plastic material, natural rubber, wood and wood products, electronic goods, organic chemicals, edible oils, fertilizers, etc. ASEAN countries, particularly, Malaysia, Singapore and Thailand, are increasingly investing in India in sectors such as telecommunications, fuels, hotel and tourism services, heavy industry, chemicals, fertilizers, textiles, paper and pulp, and food processing etc.(Maharana, 2007)

ASEAN-India cooperation covers a wide field, which includes Trade & Investment, Science & Technology, Tourism, Human Resource Development, Transport & Infrastructure, and Health and Pharmaceuticals. In Human Resource Development, India has imparted training to ASEAN member countries, especially Cambodia, Laos, Myanmar and Vietnam and undertaken training courses for 48 personnel from these countries for Railway training in Civil Infrastructure, Signaling Operations, and Railway Management (Department of Commerce, 2006).

India signed a Comprehensive Economic Cooperation Agreement (CECA) with Singapore in 2005. This was the first ever CECA that India signed with any Southeast Asian countries. With India-Singapore CECA coming into effect, tariff barriers between India and Singapore on a wide range of goods will be eliminated or reduced substantially. Investors and service suppliers will receive national treatment in each other's country. Standards and technical regulations in the two countries will be mutually recognized. Three Singaporean banks will be allowed to operate in India almost like any Indian bank. These measures are expected to expand the volume of India-Singapore trade and cause large investments to flow between the two countries. India welcomes Singaporean investment in several areas, including, importantly, infrastructure and also small and medium industries (Athukorala, 2006). The two countries cooperate with each other in knowledge-intensive industries, science and technology and education. India is able to meet, to a large extent, the demand for technically qualified professionals in Singapore. The presence of young Indian professionals in Singapore is a witness of growing partnership which many believe is the only country in Southeast Asia with whom India truly has "Strategic Partnership".

India has negotiated a free trade agreement (FTA) with Thailand for setting up of a free trade area covering goods, services and investment in 10 years. The Indo-Thai FTA covers as many as 84 items and several areas in the first phase including services, investment, economic cooperation and goods like food items, tourism, auto parts, and electronic goods. As a part of economic diplomacy to promote bilateral relations, both India and ASEAN decided to have Free Trade Agreement in the Second India-ASEAN summit in 2002 in Bali. Due to different technical reasons it could not become a reality in the initial period. One of the major berries is the huge size of negative list that India maintained. Though India has downsized its negative list, still some difficulties are there on palm oil, MFN status etc (Kumar, 2006).

Despite the difficulties both India and ASEAN signed FTA in 2010 in goods and during the commemorative Summit in 2012, December, it has been extended to services sector and investment. Following the India-ASEAN FTA trade between the two grew by 41% in 2011-12.

During the commemorative Summit held in December, 2012 in New Delhi, India ASEAN relation reached a new high. Both celebrated twenty years of dialogue partnership and ten years of summit partnership. The summit adopted a vision statement that elevated the relationship to strategic partnership with emphasis on economic agreements achievement on prolonged connectivity between the two regions and determination to work together towards building a stable and peaceful regional order.

North-East India in the Framework of Look-east Policy

With the process of liberalization initiated in India under structural adjustment programme since 1991, Indian economy has achieved tremendous growth prospects. It has led to the entry of foreign capital, expansion of Indian trade beyond domestic boundaries, growth in service sector and resultant generation of employment opportunities etc. Above all India now stands among the fast moving nation states of the world economic giants. However, India's projected growth path which India moves is not free from its on inherent limitations. The macro-economic trends show high level of regional imbalance and socio economic backwardness since the inception of economic liberalization. India's North-East region is one of prime the examples of it. (Das and Barua, 1996)

Following the India ASEAN FTA Trade between the two groups by 41% in 2011-12.

Policy makers are attempting to remedy the economic backwardness of the region. Most of the states in the region are unable to generate their own revenues to meet their expenses. These are some prime reasons of growing extremism within the region. The region is land locked and connected to the mainland India only with the 22kms long corridor knows as 'chicken neck'. (Sachedeva, et.al., 2000)

The location of the region, comprises states of Arunachal Pradesh, Assam, Manipur, Meghalaya, Mizoram, Nagaland, Tripura and Sikkim. North-East is strategically important as it has international borders with Bangladesh, Bhutan, China, Myanmar and Tibet. The area is characterized by rich bio-diversity, endowed with forest wealth and is ideally suited to produce a whole range of plantation crops, spices, fruits, vegetables, flowers and herbs. The rich natural beauty, serenity and exotic flora and fauna of the area are invaluable resources for the development of eco-tourism. Total area of the region is about 2, 55,168 Sq. Km. All the seven states are members of the North East Council (NEC) which was formed on 1st August 1972. (Puri, 1998)

The region has a high concentration of tribal population. The states of Arunachal Pradesh, Meghalaya, Mizoram and Nagaland are mostly inhabited by a number of native tribes. Each tribe has its own distinct tradition of art, culture, dance, music and life styles. The numerous fairs and festivals celebrated by these communities and their friendly nature are irresistible attractions for the visitors. (Bezbaruah, 2001)

The North East is one of the most ethnically and linguistically diverse regions in India. Each of the seven states that form this part of India has its own culture and tradition. Assam occupies the lush lowlands of the Brahmaputra Valley and is the most densely populated. Arunachal Pradesh occupies the densely forested and sparsely populated foothills of the Himalayas, and is one of the major tourist attractions because of its Buddhist influence. Meghalaya, with its pine clad hills and lakes, is famous as the wettest region of the world. Nagaland has a rich war history that attracts tourists. The other three states – Manipur, known as the 'land of jewels', Mizoram and Tripura make up a fascinating area consisting of green valleys, lush hills with variety of flora and fauna. (Bandopadhaya, 2007).

The entire North-East India remains security sensitive due to various aspects of insurgency some of which have cross-border dimension. While in Nagaland the parallel governance is a major cause for concern, Assam, Manipur, Meghalaya and Tripura on the other hand continue to witness acts of violence. Although the system of institutional democracy is found to see in the North-Eastern region with periodic elections the security issues have continued to overshadow the prospects of economic development (Hazarika, 1996).

India shares 1643 km long border with Myanmar that passes through the northeastern states of Arunachal Pradesh, Manipur, Mizoram and Nagaland. Although cross-border contact and movement of people are known throughout history, they have not led to any strong economic inter-dependence between the regions across the border so far. Lack of infrastructure is one of the major reasons for this. However, the end of Cold War and the onset of economic globalization are generating new atmosphere for inter-regional economic cooperation which is needed to harness growth in the states of the North-East. Neither the strategic geographical location of the North-East India, nor the region's similarity with the countries of Southeast Asia in cultural and ethnic terms can be ignored. Many of the communities of the Northeast India have their origin in the Southeast Asian region. Acoording to Sanjib Baruah , "North-East India's isolation from its neighborhood has much older roots: that which came about as a result of the advent of western dominance over sea routes and over global trade and more particularly the British conquest of the region and decisions to draw lines between the hills and plains, to put barriers if trade between Bhutan and Assam and to treat Myanmar as a strategic frontier – British India's buffer against French Indonesia and China. While the British colonial rulers built a major new transportation infrastructure, aimed primarily at taking tea and other resources out of Assam, the disruption of old trade route remained colonialism's most enduring negative legacy." (Baruah, 2005)

In the recent past, there has been much talk to make North-east India as a gateway of ASEAN. Number of initiatives has been taken by the Ministry of External Affairs, Ministry of Industry and Commerce, and Ministry of Development of the North-Eastern Region (DoNER). Workshops and Seminars are a common occurrence now.. Steps like opening of the Stilwel road, trade through Tamu region in Manipur have already started. Talks are going on Trans Asian railway. The ASEAN-India car rally in 2004 was flagged off in Guwahati with much expectation. It was flagged off by Prime Minister Dr. Manmohan Singh at Guwahati on 22 November, 2004. The Rally concluded at Batam, Indonesia on 11 December, 2004. The rally lasting for a period of 20 days travelled through 11 countries covering approximately 8,000 km (Assam Tribune, 2004). It has evoked considerable public interest in North-East India and ASEAN countries. India will showcase its business potential in its northeastern states during a four-day mega bazaar in Thailand in October, 2007, part of a major campaign to open the region to investors in Southeast Asia (www.ipcs.org/countResearchPaper). The central ministry of the Department of North Eastern Region (DoNER) in collaboration with the Indian Chamber of Commerce (ICC) has organized the North East Investment Week in Bangkok. The ongoing phase of India's Look-East policy is emphasizing much on its North-East region. Borders are seen not as boundaries but as gateways to opportunities and of international trade and commerce (Verghese 2004).

The economic integration of the North-East India with the ASEAN region will bring prosperity and stability to the region. This will enable it to liberate itself from present landlocked status. Economic advantages that will follow on if linked with the booming economies of the Southeast Asian countries. The share of trade of the North-East in the annual trade with ASEAN countries is estimated to be 12 percent. On March 23, 2007, Thai Chamber of Commerce and Broad of Trade of Thailand in association with the Indian embassy in Bangkok hosted a meeting on 'Emerging Opportunities between India and Thailand' with focus on North-Eastern region of India.

However, in the interest of North-East, it needs to be emphasized that indigenous industrial production like agriculture, handicraft, handloom, tea etc has to be encouraged. Tourism may prove to be prospective area. But for it to be successful infrastructure, easy connectivity are essential. Otherwise it will remain only a transit for trade without proving long term benefits to the "neglected region" (Alokesh Baruah, 2005). Region's being part of India's economic success would help in winning over the dissidents and in feeling pride in being equal partners in India's growing image as a future "super power".

Table 1.1: India-ASEAN Export Trade

Section	1993-95	1996-98	1999-01
1	2	3	4
Live animal	2,903.50	7,528.00	6,584.20
Vegetables	145,792.90	260,410.60	636,597.20
Oil products	763,817.80	2,420,726.30	3,371,487.70
Prepared food stuffs	129,619.90	195,898.00	168,600.30
Mineral products	1,083,364.70	1,890,812.60	3,000,750.00
Plastics	216,299.00	596,269.60	562,429.40
Leathers	6,569.00	13,255.80	22,123.50
Wood articles	110,679.50	218,517.70	566,859.40
Pulp and paper	109,284.00	253,859.30	346,043.10
Textile	168,124.60	308,717.00	549,616.10

(Table Contd...)

1	2	3	4
Footwear	5,802	4,537.70	12,323
Stone/cement	72,568.60	108,286.20	129,142.40
Gems	168,438.00	512,378.20	319,503.80
Metal article	644,439.90	679,667.20	782,474.20
Machinery products	1,525,384.90	3,322,374.60	5,223,592.70
Vehicles	291,744.60	762,122.20	315,839.90
Precious instruments	155,355.90	284,607.90	369,588.50
Arms	2.80	52.60	10.40
Miscellaneous article	25,634.50	40,039.40	63,158.30
Works of art	166,728.00	360,566.40	255,466.20
Chemicals	501,850.90	991,278.10	1603,700.00
Other	131.20	181,957.50	37,855.80
Total	6,294,536.80	13,413,861.00	18,343,746.60

Source: Ariff and Cheen,(2006), ASEAN Secretariat (2003)

Table 1.2: India-ASEAN Import Trade

Section	1993-95	1996-98	1999-01
1	2	3	4
Live animal	215,250.20	697,285.50	594,842.40
Vegetables	348,889.00	881,837.40	557,542.10
Oil products	7,804.70	22,864.60	35,114.40
Prepared food stuffs	633,610.90	1,250,931.00	721,440.80
Mineral products	232,212.00	1,478,436.80	446,917.20
Plastics	206,966.00	131,389.50	187,330.30
Leathers	63,067.60	57,824.10	69,110.30
Wood articles	12,088.40	9,627.70	10,331.90
Pulp and paper	30,223.10	38,594.60	57,185.80

(Table Contd...)

1	2	3	4
Textile	575,812.30	756,985.50	660,248.90
Footwear	18,855	35,077.10	21,315
Stone/cement	68,047.30	100,256.70	74,804.60
Gems	314,303.20	371,171.20	872,486.50
Metal article	723,201.80	789,807.80	1,006,899.30
Machinery products	743,856.40	1,241,956.50	2,039,780.80
Vehicles	115,000.50	183,148.50	152,338.00
Precisious instruments	21,211.60	76,709.50	77,292.50
Arms	9.90	74.00	442.90
Miscellaneous article	22,107.40	21,780.60	25,937.70
Works of art	33,317.90	48,629.40	49,375.50
Chemicals	428,121.70	790,425.60	1,298,439.50
Other	1,105.30	4,867.80	9,119.40
Total	4,815,062.00	8,989,681.40	8,968,295.70

Source: Ariff and Cheen, (2006), ASEAN Secretariat (2003)

2

Geo-strategic and Historical Significance of North-East India vis-a-vis ASEAN Region

Introduction

Geography and political factors have made the North-Eastern region into a far away land, remote, isolated and surrounded by intimidating and unsympathetic environment. Despite richly endowed in resources, the region has brought into the category of what is called "backward". The partition of the country made it a remote frontier connected to the mainland by a narrow 22 km Siliguri corridor and caused economic, social and political isolation. Tendency to assert independent "nationalities" and identities from rising ethno-cultural consciousness of various groups, has led to a climate of violence, lawlessness and insurgency. The inhospitable neighbourhood and pressures from unregulated migration form neighbouring countries – particularly Bangladesh, have added to the tension. All the above and remoteness from the markets combined with poor infrastructure and weak governance have kept the private investments away, creating a stagnant economy. Verghese, (2001) mentions that the people of the region would like to have peace and progress leading to prosperity and peace. They would also like to march on the path of economic, social and cultural progress and equity. They would like to see inclusive economic growth with equal opportunities for a secure living and future with dignity and self respect. Moving far away from the dependency syndrome, where the people have to seek and look up to the gratis from the distant land, the people in the region would like to acquire confidence and capabilities to shape their own destinies. They would like to achieve economic prosperity and engage in global competition while retaining their distinct and rich regional and ethnic identities.

In this chapter an analysis of the geo-political importance of North-East India, its strategic location vis-à-vis the ASEAN region will be undertaken. The foreign policy makers of the country see North-East India as the bridge between India and Southeast Asia. The study will also cover traditional and cultural connectivity of North-East India with that of Southeast Asia. Historical significance is another effective factor in making North-East India a gateway to ASEAN.

Demography and Social-Economic Structure

The Northeastern region comprises of eight states and these cover an area of 255000 sq. km constituting 7.9 percent of total geographical area of India as per the 2001 census. More than 68 per cent of the population of the region lives in the state of Assam alone. The density of population varies from 13 per sq. km in Arunachal Pradesh to 340 in Assam. The major hilly terrain in all the states except Assam has an overwhelming proportion of tribal population. It is ranging from 19.3 per cent in Assam to 94.5 per cent in Mizoram. There are about 635 tribal communities. The region is predominantly rural with over 80 per cent of the population living in the villages. According to the 2001 Census, the literacy rates of the population in the region are 68.5 per cent and 61.5 per cent respectively in Assam and Mizoram which were higher than the national average. More significantly, the literacy rate has not translated in terms of higher employability or productivity. With huge natural resources, the region is identified as one of the world's biodiversity hotspots. The tropical rain forests are favourable for diverse flora and fauna and several crop species. The forest cover in the region constitutes 52 per cent of the total geographical area. Reserves of petroleum and natural gas in the region constitute a fifth of the country's total potential. The region is covered by the Ganga - Brahmaputra – Meghna river systems and small rivulets. (Pramanik, Bimal , 2006)

The standard of living of the people has lagged behind the rest of the country in 2004-05, the region's per capita income was Rs. 18027 which was less than the all-state average of Rs. 25,968. The available information shows that at the time of independence per capita income in the undivided state of Assam was higher than the national average by 4 per cent (NER Vision 2020). The growth rate of per capita Gross State Domestic Product has also lagged behind the rest of the country. With the ushering of market based economic reforms, the differences in the growth rates in per capita Gross State Domestic product between the region and the country has increased. From, 1990-91 to 2004-05, on average, while the aggregate Gross State Domestic product of all states in constant prices increased at 6 per cent per year, the corresponding growth in the region was 4.4 per cent. Similarly, the region's growth rate of per capita income (2.5%) lagged behind the average growth rate of the country (4%) during the 1990-91 to 2004-05 by 1.5 percentage points. Not surprisingly, the difference in the per capita incomes between the country and the region has steadily diverged (NER Vision 2020). In 1990-91, the region's per capita income in current prices was lower than the country average by 20 per cent and this difference increased to 31 per cent by 2004-05. (Umdor, 2007).

The states within the North East region carry intra-states variation in terms of their economies. Except for Mizoram, Nagaland and Sikkim which recorded marginally higher growth rate than the country average. Per capita income levels in all other states were lower by varying magnitudes. Assam, the largest among the North-Eastern states had the lowest per capita income at Rs. 15,661 which was lower than the country's average by 40 per cent. In fact, the share of income generated by the public administration sector at 10.6 per cent was significantly higher in the region than in the country (NER,

Vision 2020). It was over 17 per cent in Arunachal Pradesh, Manipur and Sikkim. This underlines the overwhelming dependence of the population on the government for generating incomes due to lack of productive economic activities in primary, secondary and tertiary sectors of the economy. The region lags behind in comparison to rest of the country as evident from development indicators. People do not have access even to basic services in adequate measures. The standard development indicators such as road length, access to healthcare and power consumption in the region are below the national average.

The region has less than 8 per cent of its 63257 MW of hydroelectric power generation potential and the per capita power consumption in the region at 117 kwh is less than a third of the national average (373 kwh). In Manipur and Nagaland, the per capita power consumption is as low as 73 Kwh and 61 Kwh respectively and in Assam, it is 104 Kwh. The literacy rate in the region is high, but the capacity of the population to engage in productive economic activities is low (Subba and Ghosh, 2003). The incidence of poverty in the region is high. Besides, the calorie requirement in these areas is higher and the area is also handicapped by higher cost of living than the plains.

One of the main reasons for such backwardness lies in the development strategy itself. The trickle down development planning strategy has not involved people in designing and implementing the development strategy Lack of people's involvement has robbed the system a sense of belonging and has led to inefficient and wasteful resource allocation on the one hand and lack of social accountability on the other and this has only added to the sense of frustration and a breeding ground for insurgency. In this context Verghese (2006) argues that the economic stagnation in the region must be attributed to the structural damage caused by the partition. The blockade of transportation routes and markets and insulation of the economy caused structural damage by isolating the economy and the people, blocking the natural transportation routes, hindering the development of markets, creating a dependency syndrome and spreading the culture insurgency. With poor penetration of the markets and development, not based on the resources of the region, the planning process hardly created any scope for developing forward and backward linkages with the economy.

The weak administrative capacity of the state has resulted in armed insurgency and the widespread incidence of roving banditry. These have proved to be a major deterrent to the economic investment by private sector. In addition, the capacity of the institutions of market as well as governance in the region is weak and unresponsive. The poor incentive structure caused by policies and institutions has further contributed to the adverse impact on the development process.

Geo-Strategic Importance of North-East India

The geography of a country with its fraternity, climate, and location in relation to land and water ways influence country's foreign policy to a great extent. It provides self – sufficiency to a country. Land-locked countries, nations situated in the tropical area, those bordering superpower are less self-sufficient in comparison to the countries located in the temperate areas far away from the superpowers (Kumar, 1967). India's geo-strategic position in South Asia enables her to be a major power in the region. Describing India's strategic location Nehru had said in 1949:

> *"Look at the map. If you have to consider any question affecting the Middle East, India inevitably comes into the picture. If you have to consider any question concerning South-East Asia, you cannot do so without India. So also with the Far-East. While the Middle East may not be directly connected with South-East Asia, both are connected with India. Even if you think in terms of regional organization in India you have to keep in touch with the other region."* (Dixit, Ramesh, 1998)

Nehru's comment may not have mentioned North East India but it is a fact that India's land connectivity with Southeast Asia is through North-East emerges. The region stretches down from the foothills of the Himalayas in the eastern range and is surrounded by Bangladesh, Bhutan, China and Myanmar. It includes the seven sisters - Arunachal Pradesh, Assam, Manipur, Meghalaya, Mizoram, Nagaland and Tripura along with a small and beautiful cousin in the Himalayan fringes namely, Sikkim. According to Verghese (2004), the region is a "rainbow country: extraordinarily diverse and colourful, mysterious when seen through parted clouds, a distant and troubled frontier for all too many". Rich in natural resources and balanced bio–diversity, the region was a gateway to East and Southeast Asia before independence. It was well connected with the Southeast Asian region through the historical silk route and Chittagong port. But the partition by the British in 1947 made the region land locked. After the partition the Chittagong port went to East Pakistan which eventually became Bangladesh. Troubled by history and geo-politics, the Northeast has remained one of the most backward regions of the country. Partition of the country in 1947 placed the region economically backward position and blocked the ways for future progress. It isolated the region heartland and sealed both land and sea routes for commerce and trade (Hazarika, 1996).

Geographically, apart from Brahmaputra, Barak and Imphal valleys and some flat lands in between the hills of Meghalaya and Tripura, the remaining two-thirds area of the region consists of hilly terrain. The rich endowment of resources is accompanied by a fascinating history of prosperity and progress. The large river systems and small rivulets provided a means of livelihood for the vast majority of the population in the valleys and plains. Driven by expanding trade and investment, the region was in the forefront of development almost 150 years ago. The global trade was conducted through the sea route through Chittagong, and land transportation through roads and railways. The railway network between Dibrugarh and Chittagong was one of the earliest projects in India implemented by the British in the late 19th century. While the road to the north from Gangtok and Agartala established the 'Silk Route' for trade with China, the port town of Chittagong served as the gateway for tea trade. The natural transportation route through East Bengal not merely reduced the physical distance but brought emotional closeness (Prabhakara, 2004). The region witnessed rapid spread of tea gardens with the first garden in 1835. The export of tea to London which started in 1838 brought employment and prosperity to the people of the region in the subsequent period of time. The discovery of oil in Makum and establishment of a refinery in Digboi in 1890 laid the foundation for the development of undivided Assam. The unnatural bifurcation of the boundaries and the partition of the country in 1947 changed the entire economic landscape of the region completely. The geo-political isolation of the region from the country combined with economic insulation caused immense structural damage to the North-East India's economy. Baruah (2005), states that the partition made the system virtually land-locked and blocked the natural transportation routes and severed market access to the region. Political fragmentation of the region, quest for ethnic and regional identity and nationalism, ideological motivations and more recently religious fundamentalism have created a climate of insurgency in several parts of the Northeastern region. There is a feeling of dissatisfaction as a result of what is perceived as lack of development.

The states of Arunachal Pradesh, Nagaland, Manipur and Mizuram share 1,643 km border on their east with Myanmar (Srivastava, 1987). The state-centric security perception, both in India and Myanmar, treated this border as vulnerable periphery. India's attempts to isolate Myanmar in 80s and 90s affected the North East border security when narcotic smugglings and cross border insurgency increased rapidly. Moreover, China entered into this political vacuum by establishing strong military ties with Myanmar. In the northeast part of Myanmar, China has a long border of 2185 km. Thailand's border of 1,800 km also runs along the eastern part of Myanmar. Myanmar provides easy access to most of the ASEAN countries. The location of Myanmar is such that the two Asian powers India and China want to have a major influence. It is in this context India's North-Eastern region gains significant importance in country's foreign policy initiation due to its strategic closeness with Myanmar (Singh, 2006).

Steps have been taken to build connectivity. The government of Assam, in 2007, opened up the Stilwell road which connects Ledo in Assam and Kunming in China via Myanmar. The opening of the road as expected to bring tremendous trade opportunities to both North-East India in particular and India as a whole. Trade prospects and other related issues associated with the Stilwell road will be discussed in the next chapter.

Connectivity

The demography of North East India reflects that the original people of the region are mostly hilly people. According to some sources these hilly people were Austroloid. They used to call their land as Pagar-Juh-Tish in their language. In earliest period, their societies were matriarchal. In course of time, successive migrations of Mongoloid people from the regions of Far East and Southeast Asia took place due to different reasons and assimilated with the Austroloid origin of Assamese people. Through the Mongoloid tradition of intermarriage among the tribes, difference between the Austroloid and Mongoloid became thinner and accordingly, the Austroloids marged into the Mongoloid tribes (Gogoi, 2004). In this process of assimilation the tribes of North East India maintained an influence of Far East and Southeast Asia in different aspects. Here the focus is basically on lingual, cultural and traditional aspects. For example the Tai-Ahom community, once the ruling community and one of the dominant ethnic groups in the North East India, has its origin in Thai race which is presently found in the different parts of China, South and Southeast Asia. (Taher, 1993)

(a) Lingual Connectivity

The main linguistic branches of Mongloid origin found in the North Eastern region of India are the Sino-Tibetan and

Tibeto-Burman. They entered into the present North-East India in the period prior to 2000 B.C. In the whole region of Brahmputra valley, there evolved a number of linguistic groups which were branches of the larger Sino Tibetan language. According to Prof. Tan-Chung both the linguistic groups can be sub- divided. This is like Sino- Tibetan as Tibeto and Sino –Tai, and Tibeto Burman as Tobeto Himalayan, North Assam and Assam Burman. In the North East region commonly found groups are North Assam and Assam Burman (Baruah, 1976).

It is mentioned in the leaflet published by Tai-Ahom Council (1988) that the main dialects which come under the North Assam branch are Adi, Missing, Nishi, Dafala, and Misimi. These dialects have their local variations such as Wansu, Tangsa, Singphu, Bathin, Khamsa, Lap- nan, Kaiman, Lap-lang, Bun-ting, Khesla, Lamsa, Tupi, Pulung, Kheti, Thin-sa, Kapu, Bera, Hun- khan, Dadom, Mokotua, Edu, Kaman,Yera-Un, Padam, Khemti etc for better communication in the village areas.

The main language come under Assam Burman branch is Boro-kachari. It has several sub branches such as Deuri, Chutia, Boro, Kachari, Gari, Rabha, Diamasa, Tiwa, Koch, Karbi, Mech Tipra, Maran, Hojai, Sonowal, Jharo, Thengal etc. In Nagaland various tribes are found speak in Assam Burman language. There are fourteen such branches are found in Nagaland. They are mainly Kanyak, Angami, Ao, Sema, Lutha, Chekhe Chang, Phum, Rengha, Sengh-tam, Pachuri, etc. They have their sub branches also. (Terwiel, 1973)

Another group of languages comes under Assam Burman branch is Kuki-Chin. It comprises of Lusai that is Mizo, Hmer, Paite, Pawi, Lakher, Hrangkhawl, Vaiphei, Khelma, Kuki, Blahte, etc. These languages have many similarities with each other. The Kuki-Chin group has many similarities with the Sino-Tai language group (Gogoi, 1968).

The main languages under Sino-Tai branch are Meitei of Manipur and Mizo of Mizoram. Other sub-branches of Sin-Tai group are Tai-Kham-Ti, Tai-Phake, Tai Ahom, Tai-

Khamyang, Tai-Turung and Tai-Aiton and Tai-Ahom. Except Tai-Ahom all other languages are spoken in the Southeast Asian region. The Sino –Tai group of languages are spoken with some variations in the part of China, Myanmar, Laos, Cambodia, Vietnam, Thailand, and in some part of Pacific Island. Many of these languages are also known to their origin in the Shan-Tai of Tai-Shan group. They are Tai Khamti, Tai Kham Yang, Tai Phake, Tai Turung, and Tai Ahom (Guha, 1977). There are minor differences among them. But though they have differences in dialects and languages, yet these mongoloid groups maintain a cultural unity among themselves. The historic Tai-Ahom rule of six hundred years since form the 1228 A.D. played the most significant role in creating this cultural unity among these different Mongoloid groups. The continuous rule of Tai-Ahoms till 1826A.D brought all these Mongoloid tribes under the one socio-political umbrella. It became possible for the Tai-Ahoms to shape this process as the different ethnic groups shared a common Mongoloid food habit, moral values and homogenous social fabric (Baruah, B.K, 1954). Here it becomes necessary to discuses the Tai-Ahom history, its cultural linkages with Southeast Asia. It is particularly important as this ethnic group of Mongoloid origin of East and Far-East played all possible efforts to build a unified Assam (present North East India).

(b) The Tai-Ahoms: A Brief Overview

The Tai-Ahoms of North East India have their roots in the Shan branch of great Tai race. This Tai race ruled in ancient China and known as 'Chung-kuo'. They are presently found in different parts of China, and Southeast Asia. The Thai (Tai) history began with the process of formation of tribal polity on the banks of the rivers Hwang-ho and Yang-tze. These were stateless societies which in the course of time migrated to the different places in South and Southeast and assimilated with the socio-political conditions in these new societies. Over the years they have forgotten some of their customs and traditions. They maintained a tradition of making it mandatory for the royal families to rear silk worms. Their grew princely monopoly over the silk art and its production, which eventually attracted traders of the west. This led to the construction of silk roads for the export purposes (Baruah, G.C, 1987). Reference can be made to the historical Silk Road connecting India's North-East and China via Southeast Asia which had been major means of trade untill the British period.

The Tai-Ahoms established their kingdom in the North East India region in the 13th century under their king Hsu-Ka-Pha. They called their land as 'Mung-Dum-Sun-Kham'. This is the land which is today known as Assam. According to the historical sources Hsu-Ka-Pha entered Assam in 1228 A.D. with some of his chiefs and three priestly families along with 9000 followers. Hsu-Ka-Pha entered North East through the 'Eastern Silk Road' across the Patkai ranges (Goswami, Hemchanda, 1922). This road was later developed by Capt. Stilwell during the Second World War, and is today known as 'Stilwell Road'. It connects Ledo in Assam and Kunming in China via the Shan state of Myanmar. The road is very important from the point view of India's Look East policy as it provides tremendous trade opportunities with cheap transportation. It also provides easy access to the economies of not only Southeast Asia but also to China and Hongkong. Considering its significance the road has been re-opened recently.

Hsu-Ka-Pha (Sukapha) established his kingdom in the Brahmaputra valley. It is from the Tribal name of Ahom, the Brahmaputra valley came to be known as Assam. The Ahoms have contributed much toward the development of the Assamese society and virtually absorbed the Hindu social structure.

The Ahoms were free from religious inhibitions and caste prejudices. They were more practical and tolerant of others. They gradually came under the influence of the Aryan culture and became patrons of it and contributed to the composite growth of the Assamese identity. Since they were liberal and also due to the low sex ratio of women, the Ahoms married non-Ahom, Aryan girls. Though it provided the way for the assimilation of the Ahom and non-Ahom culture, it did not mean that the Ahoms completely abandoned their tradition. Although since the fourteenth century, a larger section of the Tai-Ahoms started adopting Hindu customs, three of the priestly classes Mohan, Deodhai and Bailung remained outside the influence of Hinduism and continued to profess their own culture and rituals. Even today they are maintaining their own Tai culture (Barua, 1977).

Agriculture was the main source of living during the Ahom's time. Rice was the major crop cultivated. Cultivation of rice was one of the major factors responsible for creating cultural identities and social values of the Ahoms. The rites and folk lore related to the rice cultivation reflect the Tai culture in the traditional Ahom society. The festival of 'Chang Can' of the Thai cultivators and 'Bihu' of the Ahoms are the manifestation of the agrarian culture. The ceremonies like farm land fertilizing, first rice growing, rite to get rid of paddy inflictions are similar to the ceremonies performed by the Thai farmers of other countries particularly of Siamese of central Thailand. Terwiel, (1983) argues that the ploughing instruments used by the Ahoms are almost similar to that of the Tais in the different parts of Southeast Asia. The Ahoms used bamboo extensively like the Tais of Southeast Asia. Bamboo was used to make fencing, in fishing equipment, tools of handlooms etc.

Gogoi (1968) mentions a number of other rituals of Ahoms which have impact of Thai imprint. The Ahoms performed the ceremony of 'Rik Khan' which is also found in Thailand. This festival is observed to gain longevity. The Ahoms performed this ceremony on the occasions when a person has had severe shock or fight and also during marriage ceremonies. Almost similar type of ceremony known as 'Riak Khawan' in Thai language is performed in the northern part of Thailand.

Like the traditional Tai people, the Ahoms also constructed their houses with wood, bamboo. The peculiar Ahoms houses which is known as 'Huam Ram' or 'Chang Ghar' in popular term, with about two metres above the ground level, resembles the construction of the Tais of Southeast Asia. Such houses were built to protect them from the attack of wild animals and enemies. (Nartsupha, Chatthip, 2002)

Ahoms in the rural areas still maintaining their traditional food habits. Rice is the main food and 'Nam-Lao' (home made rice beer) is the traditional drink. Besides they prepare a number of food items from rice quite similar to the Tais of Southeast Asia. These are 'Handhaguri' (a kind of specially prepared fried rice), 'Chunga Chawal'(rice cooked in the immature bamboo pipes), Til Pitha (a special item prepared from sticky rice powder), Kumal Chawal (unboiled soft rice), Tupula Bhat (a kind of packed rice) etc. Like the Thais, the Ahoms prefer to take boiled food without spice, burnt fish and vegetables, espisially brinjal.

The dress style of Ahoms also reflects many aspects of their social setting. As traditional dresses are identified with group identity, the Ahoms are maintaining it. The character of textiles such as woven dresses made from cotton and Muga silk reflect the imprint of thai textile culture among the Ahoms. They are adept in making thread from Muga and Edi-worms. This practice of sericulture and rearing Eri worms is almost similar to the traditional Tai societies in the Southeast Asia and China. The rural Ahom men wear 'Dhuti' and a particular shirt made of Muga silk. The Ahom women wear 'Mekhela' woven with Muga silk, 'Seleng sadar' and 'Reha' (Terwiel, 1980).

The Ahoms have a collective work culture. People in the rural area stand united in the time of marriage ceremonies, in building houses and during harvesting time. Connectivity is also seen at the time of fishing, hunting etc. Significantly, when social customs based on caste, creed, were highly predominant among the people of Aryan origin, it was almost absent among the Ahoms. They maintained and are still maintaining a high degree of prestige and self respect. They are simple by nature and are very hospitable.

The Tai Ahoms follow a tradition which has a clear impact of Confucianism (Sahai, Sachchidanand, 2002). They allow the eldest son of the family to perform all the duties of a father in his absence. The sons and daughters of the elder brother are always regarded as elder irrespective of their age. The Tai-Ahoms observe a customary marriage ritual which is called 'Chalk Long' in their language. The 'Chalk Long' system originated with the evolution of Tai race in the East and Southeast Asia. The original Tai-Ahom term for Chalklong was 'Song-Leng' which subsequently got changed to 'Chalk-Long' in Assamese language. In Tai 'Song' means 'two' and 'Leng' means 'one'. So 'Song-Leng' indicates the unification of two souls.

The Ahom kings were called 'Swargadeo'. In Assamese swarga means heaven. The Tai people regarded their kings as sacred and so the Ahom kings were given the title of 'Chou-Pha', means 'the son of Heaven'. The Tai people believed that the king rules the subjects for the welfare of the subjects as they had the mandate from the Heaven. The royal families of Ahoms claim their descent form 'Lengdon' means the lord of heavenly kingdom 'Tien-Kuo', who sent his grandsons Khunlung and Khunlai to establish their kingdom. That's why they worshiped Pha Lengdom. The Ahoms perform 'Um-Pha, a kind of special worship at an interval of 12 years. It was first performed on the 'Sarai Doi Hills' after the advent of Su-Ka-Pha, the first Ahom king in Assam. Su-Ka-Pha performed Um-Pha when he entered the soil of North-East India with a view of praying Tao, the heavenly god of Tais for his blessings on the establishment of his kingdom in Assam. The tradition in this sacrifice is to offer a white elephant, a white buffalo and a white cow among other things for sacrifice. The origin of this animal sacrifice has a long history connected with the Tai believe (Gogoi, 1968).

'Me-Dam-Me- Phi' is another custom connected with ancestral worship of the Ahoms. Its origin is traced to a long cultural and historical process involving in the formation of the Tai races in the Southeast Asia. This custom reflects the

principles of 'Cannon of Yao', the constitution of the Tai kingdom flourished on the banks of river Hwang- ho. This Tai constitution was framed by the fourth Tai king Yao. *Me* means offering or worship, *Dam* means a particular stage of existence after death o the Tais till they attain the status of *Phi* (deity), whereas *Phi* means a lesser god in the stage of spirit. Hence the Tai believe is that their accomplished ancestors are still living in between Heaven and Earth (Barua and Phukan, 1964)

The Tai Ahoms keep an emblem of flying dragon in their scriptures. It is a winged horse with claws of different shapes. According to Ahom scriptures, 'Phukao Kham', a goddess in charge of heaven came down to the Earth and fell in love with the God. As result of their consummtion, four eggs were created. The first egg gave birth to Chou Ai Kaw-Pha who was given the charge of Heaven. The second egg created Ching Kam Pha who became the owner of thunder and lightening. Chang Din Ngeo who became the master of eight lakh serpents, was born out from the third egg. The fourth egg gave birth to Ngi Ngao Kham who became preceptor of the Tai Phralong cult and was in charge of the Tai scriptures. Ngi-Ngao Kham took the dragon form of a flying horse. This dragon horse can fly on sky, swim in the water and walk in the earth according to the Tai myth. This flying dragon horse is still the cultural symbol of Ahoms in North-East which is also found among the Tais in Thailand (Gogoi, 1968)

This is evident that India's North-East region not only has border connectivity with the ASEAN countries but also is closely connected with the Southeast Asia in a greater historical and more cultural terms. The strategic angle has already been addressed in different policy directives. However, the political elite has to give credence to traditional and cultural linkages which will help in increasing its diplomatic ties with Southeast Asia. This factor would bring acceptability of the whole idea of making North-East India as a bridge between India and ASEAN in the region.

3

North-East India in the Framework of India-ASEAN Relations

Introduction

In 1992, when India announced its "Look-East Policy" for closer economic cooperation with ASEAN, it did not have a substantial policy on the potential of its North-East region. It is in the more recent past that India has realized the potentials of economic integration of its North-East region with that of Southeast Asia through joint economic cooperation. India is now focusing on economic integration through its North-East. It is expected that prospective development will foster the region's political integration with the mainland India.

New Delhi plans to realize the untapped economic potentials of the North-East which has resources for development of different industries such as paper, agriculture, horticulture, food processing, hydroelectrical power, gas, and oil etc. Close economic cooperation with ASEAN states will grow rapidly if India establishes connectivity between its North-Eastern states and the rest of India as well as parts of Southeast Asia. The land-locked North-East region needs to have access to the outside world which is possible only when it is linked with the ASEAN region which lies just beyond its borders (Asher, Sen, Srivastava, 2003). This will also help to give formal shape to the large external trade in the Myanmar area. Having understood the validity of this fact, New Delhi has explored the border connectivity of the North-East both through road way and sea way, with the Southeast Asian region.

If the policy has to help inclusive development, it has to directly benefit the land- locked region, otherwise the region will remain only a transit point for trade between New Delhi and Southeast Asia. Besides the central government has to consider seriously the existing ethno-cultural cum political separatist identities within the region, as well as cross-border issues such as drug abuse, human trafficking.

In this chapter main focus is on the prospects of border connectivity between New Delhi and ASEAN via North-Eastern region and various cooperative initiatives that have been taken.

An Overview

It was the war with China in 1962 that made India to take in account of the significance of its North-East as a critical frontier in its national security calculations. Chinese troops had marched down to the Brahmaputra Valley and India was clearly at a loss due to lack of critical infrastructure for faster troop deployment. After the war was over, India concentrated on building roads and military bases along the critical areas where in the past it had felt vulnerable vis-a-vis China.

The roads built at that time were targeted not towards development but were actually geared to assist India's troop deployment needs. They were never going to be enough for the genuine development of the economy of the North-East and nor were they meant for the purpose of cross-border trade (Baruah, 2002). Even for the purpose of targeted troop deployment, India clearly lagged behind China as the latter made rapid strides in building a comprehensive access infrastructure all along the border areas. Even in recent times, China has been able to build better infrastructure and has improved its ability to amass troops along the border at a short notice. The Indian policy makers in order to overcome the growing Chinese superior strength are accelerating border roads projects.

It is acknowledged fact that the North-East has not seen much development over the years, which subsequently resulted in growing feeling of seperatism and continuous cycle of violence. India has been worried about the growing threat to internal security owing to these separatist and insurgent movements. Sachdeva (2000) states that now the people of North-East India have been demanding greater connectivity with their eastern neighbourhood and particularly countries of Southeast Asia which they see as a way of greater development for their region. In this context it becomes important to examine three critical border roads that can bring development to the Northeastern states in the years to come. They are the Stilwell road or the Ledo road which connects Ledo in Assam to Kunming in Yunnan, China; the Numaligarh-Moreh road which connects the states of Assam, Nagaland and Manipur with Myanmar through the border point at Moreh; and the Aizawl-Champhai-Zowkathar road which connects Mizoram with Myanmar. Though the Moreh and Champhai outposts are being opened, official border trade through them is minimal when compared to the overall potential for trade through these corridors. Much work needs to be done in terms of proper infrastructure. The commodities allowed for trade through these two corridors also has to be expanded. A large percentage of this cross border trade through these two corridors is illegal. These corridors have also become hub for smuggling in arms and narcotics which needs to be checked through effective monitoring (Singh, T.B, 2007). Monitoring of these border roads needs coordinated effort. Hence, Confidence Building Measures (CBMs) have been taken by India especially towards Myanmar with which it had cool relation until the mid 90's.

The Assam Government has achieved one major success in the past year with the opening up of the Stilwell Road on its side of the border. This is one trade corridor which holds enormous potential for completely transforming the regional developmental dynamics of Northeast India. Built during the Second World War, the Stilwell Road has been closed since India's independence. After the reopening of the Nathu La pass, the Stilwell Road is considered as next potential step and the Indian government should keep up the expectation of its "Look-East Policy" on track.

ASEAN Car Rally

The major initiative that the government of India took to make North-East a gate way to ASEAN was the 1st India-ASEAN car rally organized on 22 November, 2004. The rally was flagged off by Prime Minister Manmohan Singh from the historic Judges Field in Guwahati in the presence of Assam Governor Lt Gen (Retd) Ajai Singh and Chief Minister Tarun Gogoi. The rally covered 8,000 kms through eight of the 10 ASEAN nations carrying the theme of "Networking People and Economies" and the objective of having a transformative effect on India-ASEAN trade and business relations (www.aseanrally.com). Nearly 250 participants from the ASEAN member countries and India participated in the rally with nearly 60 vehicles. They drove through Myanmar, Laos, Cambodia, Vietnam, Thailand, Malaysia and Singapore before culminating its 20-day journey at Batam, Indonesia, on 12 December, 2004. Prime Minister Dr. Manmohan Singh stated that the rally would play an important role in enhancing cultural and economic bonds amongst the people of the region and would also provide impetus to the development of the North-Eastern states. (Assam Tribune, 2004). In the context of the car rally the ASEAN Secretary General, in a conference held in Guwahati IIT in 2004 said that the First India-ASEAN Car Rally would open up the frontier and landlocked areas of India and ASEAN, linking our peoples at the common borders. He added "it is essential that we follow up this initial step with concrete action. I would like to offer a take-away of five "Ts" to focus the attention and action on following up today's event. The five "Ts" are: trade; tourism; training; transportation and technology" (www.aseansec.org).

The rally was jointly organized by the Ministry of External Affairs and the Confederation of Indian Industry (CII) with cooperation from ASEAN nations and the Federation of Motor Sports Clubs of India. The rally aims to create unprecedented people-to-people contact among these nations, demonstrate India-ASEAN proximity and road connectivity and promote infrastructure development, especially to facilitate road transport. The proposal for the rally was first mooted by former Prime Minister Atal Bihari Vajpayee at the ASEAN-India Summit in Bali, Indonesia, in October 2003 to bring India closer to ASEAN nations (Barbora, 2006). In accordance with the policy of focusing on the development of North-Eastern states, it was decided to flag off the rally from Guwahati. The idea behind this initiative was to create public awareness about the India-ASEAN relations, enhance trade, investment in tourism and people to people contacts.

On the occasion of 20th Commemorative year of India-ASEAN relationship, 2nd ASEAN-India use rally was organised in December, 2012 with an aim to have strong connectivity between the younger generation, entrepreneurs, technicians, media students.

"Look-East" policy or 'Indo-ASEAN Car Rally' is not meant only please neighboring countries but its own people of North-East. However, critics feel that India has to consider that North-East is not only of strategic importance for the neighboring countries but also for the nation as a whole. But the question being asked by some analysts of North-East is whether the rest of the country is aware of such position prevailing in this highly sensitive part of the country? The gap between the region and the rest of the country due to prolonged negligence has put doubt in the mind of the people regarding the intentions of the Centre.

Assam as the Gateway to Northeast and the Southeast Asia

The idea that "Assam as the gateway to the north-east and the Southeast Asia" got new shape as Prime Minister Dr. Manmohan Singh mentioned it during his inaugural speech while flagging off the ASEAN car rally on 22 November, 2004. Both the central government and state government of Assam have been working towards bringing the North-East into India's Look East Policy framework. Various efforts are being made and areas are being identified for greater economic integration with the ASEAN region. Cultural and economic linkages are given substance for the integration of North-East with the ASEAN countries. Assam has been culturally linked with the ASEAN countries for centuries and occupies the most prominent place in the Northeast. There exists a lot of potential in the region, both in terms of investment and technology, for enhanced economic relations with the ASEAN and East Asian countries.

Energy security is an important part of comprehensive engagement. Gas exploration is an important area in which the developed ASEAN countries can invest and use the latest technology. Traders and businessmen from Southeast Asia and East Asia can establish businesses here and invest in areas of potential benefits – floriculture, fisheries, food-processing, textiles, and bamboo products (Bhattacharya, 2001)

Tourism is another important area for investment in the region. Assam is very rich in terms of natural beauty, such as the mighty river, Brahmaputra, and wildlife and has scope for adventure tourism. Cultural tourism can also be an important area for cooperation since there are various historical religious places in the region representing Hinduism, Buddhism, and Christianity (Bezbaruah, 2001)

In terms of geographical proximity, North-East is nearer to ASEAN countries than to the other parts of the country whether by road or air (Ludden, 2004). The Assam government is giving importance to the Look East Policy and has taken various steps in this direction. The state government is actively participating in the meetings with ASEAN delegations in 2007, one meeting was held in New Delhi. Then subsequently it sent a delegation to Bangkok and another delegation to Singapore. Each province in North-East is focusing on those areas in which they can develop economic relations with outside players. The Assam government is focusing on jatropha plantation for bio-diesel, sericulture and also on world famous muga silk for export promotion (Assam Tribune, 2007).

- Some business companies have already started transacting and investing in the region. It will take time before more and more companies start investing, after all the companies will take sometime in investing. The Look East Policy was started in 1992 but the Northeast did not even figure in it at that time. Though the idea was there, no concrete steps were taken. It is only now after the India-ASEAN Car Rally in 2004 that the region has begun to figure in the Look East Policy.

It is difficult to say how many years it will take. Even many people in India do not know about the Look East Policy. How can we expect people from the ASEAN region to come and do business with us in one day? They first have to realize the potential of the North-East and therefore this process will take time. In fact, it is only in the last few years that the North-East has figured definitively in the Look East Policy of the country. We need to wait for all-round development. For that first, improvement of infrastructure in the region is the most important challenge. We need to develop road, rail and air linkages first among all the states of the North-East. Then we need to connect the region with mainstream India and with Southeast Asia. Second, capacity-building has to be there in every department. There is a greater necessity for capacity-building in terms of jobs, education, and skilled labour. Education is the key priority. Finally, the power situation has to be improved considerably if the region has to attract foreign traders and investment.

There is a good deal of coordination between different states of the region. But at some time there are difference which we don't discuss. But steps have to be taken to minimise intra-states difference in north-eastern region. Each state has different problems but we do not discuss them. We only discuss common policies such as industrial policy, communication policy, and so on. We expect each side to take more active role.

The Stilwell Road

The historic Stilwell Road was constructed by the Americans during the Second World War. The road connects Ledo in Assam and Kunming, China passes through Lekhapani, Jairampur, Nampong and Pangsau pass of India-Myanmar border. It starts from Patkai Range and crosses the Upper Chindwin, the Hukawng and Mogaung valleys, and goes down to Bhamo and to the Burma road which connects Kunming, Yunnan province in China.

In initial period it was called 'Ledo Road', but later it was named after the General Joseph Warren Stilwell, Chief of Staff to Allied Forces in China-Burma-India for defence of Burma (Myanmar) from Japanese forces. The Ledo road was constructed under his direct supervision during the Second World War (Steven, 1972).

Although the project of this road was prospected by British long before the Second World War it could not be implemented till the 1940's. It became possible only because of the agreement between the British and Joseph W. Stilwell who was representing the Americans on 1 December, 1942 during the Second World War when Burma was under seized by the Japanese occupation. Allied Forces required this road for restoration of line of communication between China and Burma, and a line of communication to Allied forces in Burma from India to liberate Burma from that of the Japanese forces. Lieutenant Colonel Frank D. Merrill, Operations Officer under General Stilwell, recommended building a road from Ledo, Assam, to Burma connecting the old Burma Road to provide land supply to China and Burma for support of the Allied soldiers who were fighting in North Burma. Lieutenant Colonel Frank D. Merrill had to lead a special mission with experienced jungle troops, for this dangerous and hazardous mission. He started marching with his Composite Unit from Margherita, near Ledo, India on 7 February, 1944 passing through Pangsau Pass, Shindbwlyang, Jambu-Bam, and then Myitkyi. His troop seized Myitkyina air-strip on 17 May, 1944 despite strong resistance from the Japanese forces. After some days later, they captured Myitkyina town itself, which was stronghold of Japanese forces based in north Burma. Myitkyina was one of the main missions of General Stilwell (www.geocities.com/nicchg/stiwell).

In December 1942, construction of the road began at Ledo, Assam. The Americans had brought heavy road construction machineries like bulldozers, cranes, power-shovels, caterpillars, and steam-rollers. General Stilwell had organized a 'Service of Supply' (SOS) under Major General Raymond A. Wheeler, a high profile US Army Engineer. General Wheeler was assigned to look after the construction of the Ledo road. Major General Wheeler in turn, assigned the responsibility to Colonel John C. Arrowsmith. Later, he was replaced by Colonel Lewis A. Pick, an expert US Army engineer. Road construction slowed down during the monsoon season of 1943. Even though the terrain was difficult the efforts of the finest engineers from American, Britain, India, China and West Africa succeeded in the endeavour. On 27 December, 1943, three days ahead of schedule, the road reached Shindbwiyang. The117 miles long road from Ledo to Shindbwiyang opened on 1 January, 1944 (www.tinsukia.nic.in/subpages).

In late 1944, Stilwell took the responsibility for building the difficult Ledo Road (Stilwell Road), which was connected to Burma Road. It became a highway stretching from Assam to Kunming. On 12 January, 1945, the first convoy of 113 vehicles led by General Pick started from Ledo and reached Kunming, China on 4 February, 1945 which was a great achievement. It was considered a tough task ever given to the US army engineers during Wartime. The road was renamed the Stilwell Road in honour of General Joseph Warren Stilwell at the suggestion of Chiang Kai-shek of China. The road construction was estimated to have cost 137,000,000 US dollars (Schaller, 1980).

Over the time, the Stilwell Road disappeared as it lies in three different countries China, Burma and India, due to lack of maintenance and disuse by the respective nations (Nath, 2004). Recently, India government proposed this road be reopened as International Highway linking Myanmar. In an exclusive interview then Indian Minister of State for Commerce Jairam Ramesh indicated that his Ministry would be lobbying for the reopening of Stilwell Road by 2010. Starting from Ledo in Assam to Kunming in southern China via Myitkyina in Myanmar, the road would connect India's North-Eastern states with China's southern province of Yunnan. Reopening of the road was expected to provide effective trade access to the North-East India with China and Southeast Asia.

China has expressed its interest in reopening the Stilwell Road and has already developed the Chinese stretch of the road linking it with its Super Highway No. 320. China is also involved in the development of various segments of the Stilwell Road in Myanmar. A 100 km stretch from Tengchong in Yunnan to the Warshoung in Myanmar was completed in April 2007 and 224 km segment from Myitkyina in Kachin to Tengchong is almost complete (www.assam2007blogspot.com). China is also trying for building a stretch of Stilwell road between Danai to Myitkyina in Kachin State of Myanmar. These all course have been implemented by China with its own interest.

Importantly India's friend Thailand showed its interest in the reopening of the Stilwell Road and Thailand's Deputy Industry Minister Piyabutr Cholvijarm, had during his visit to India in January 2008 appealed to New Delhi to reopen the road. However, Myanmar has not been too eager about the reopening of Stilwell. In 2004, Kyaw Dun, the Burmese Director of Border Trade, during his visit to Assam, rejected the idea of reopening Stilwell road and favoured identifying other routes to develop trade linkages between India and Southeast Asia. The military government in Myanmar has remained reluctant about the Stilwell because it passes through the Kachin State where it does not enjoy effective control (northeast.nedfi.com/blog)

Despite these national and international efforts, India is still in a dilemma over the reopening of the Road. One opinion in India believes that this would enable greater inflow of illegal arms and drugs and increased insurgent activities in the troubled region of North-East through this connectivity.

This fear is perhaps based on the experience of opening of India-Myanmar border between Moreh and Tamu. Apart from security concerns, New Delhi also has a fear that opening of Stilwell Road would turn the North-Eastern states into dumping grounds for cheap Chinese goods. However, the North-East states see the issue of opening the road in a different way, they are not worried about the China factor but see economic benefits ensuring from integrated regional infrastructure.

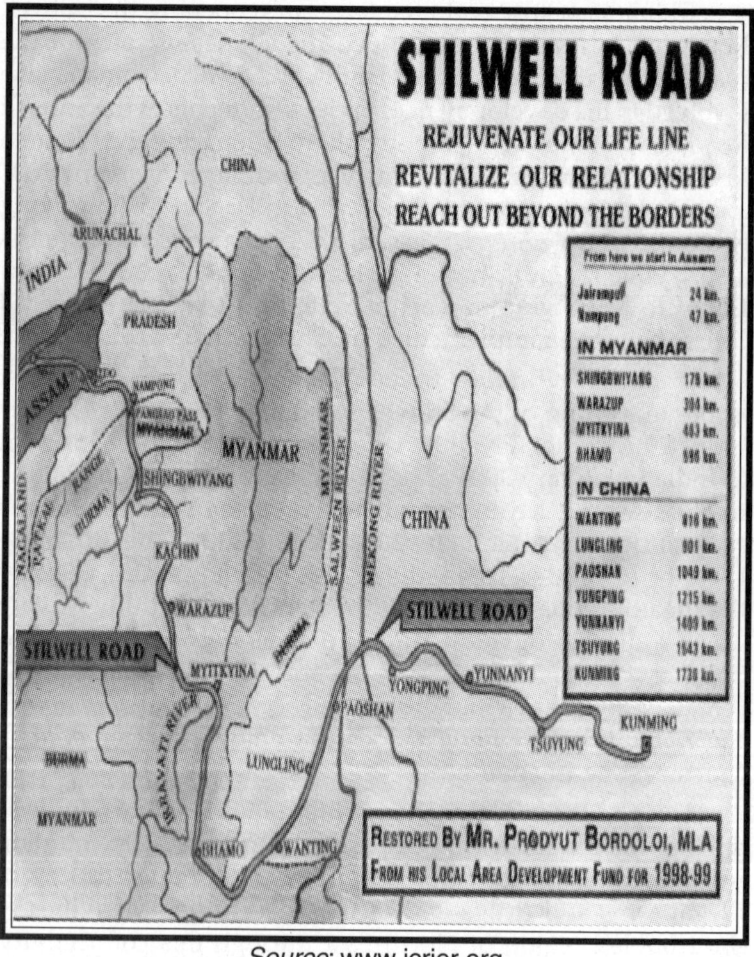

Source: www.icrier.org

Kaladan Multi-Model Transport Project

The North-East does not have a port, but it is believed that it is going to get a seaport if things go on the right track. The Government of India has planned to develop a port in Sittwe, the capital of northwest Myanmar province Rakhine (earlier known as Arakan), which is less than 400 km away from the capital of Mizoram. If the plan works out, the North-East would be connected with the port through land and river ways. Known as Kaladan multi-modal project, it includes development of Kaladan river as a waterway connecting North-East with the Bay of Bengal.

The Kaladan project will also develop connectivity between Myanmar and the North-Eastern states. Myanmar and India share a border of more than 1,600 kms, with Myanmar serves as a gateway for India to Southeast Asia and ASEAN. The project includes the upgradation of the seaport in Sittwe, widening and deepening of the Kaladan river and development of a road to connect Aizwal. The Kaladan project will include shipping, river and road transport. Moreover, with the development of Sittwe port and the Kaladan River as navigation efficient, the region is expected to be another viable access to the Southeast Asia (Lall Marie, 2006).

On April 2, 2008, Government of India signed an agreement with Myanmer Military Junta for the Kaladen project. Although the project was to begin in the end of 2009, the construction started only in November, 2010. The first and second phase of the project are being executed by state run Inland Waterways Authority of India an (RITES). But the third phase will be executed by Myanmar's Ministry of Transport. The entire project is projected to be completed by 2014-15. As per the framework agreement of 2008, Myanmar will provide land and security for the project free of charge and government of India will bear the full cost of the project. After completion project will be handed over to the government of Myanmar. It is expected that it will be used to increase trade with South-East Asia and connectivity with land-locked Mizoram. Here, one thing that government of India must ensure that the tolls going to be imposed by the Burmese government on the vessals should be affordable to the local traders of North-East India. The economy of the North-Eastern region is not that sound and financial condition of local inhabitants also does not allow to bear high tolls for using this waterway.

Minister of State for Commerce Jairam Ramesh during his visit to North-East stated: "New Delhi wants to connect North-East with the commercial sea routes. Moreover, the development of Sittwe port and the Kaladan river as connecting channels. The region will get integrate opportunities with ASEAN (Association of South East Asian Nations) nations,"(Assam Tribune, 2008). He further explained that the arrangement would allow the movement of cargo ships from Sittwe to any Indian port by using sea routes. Meanwhile, it has obtained-principle approval from the Planning Commission too (Ministry of External Affairs, 2007). The project is expected to take off after financial issues regarding its commercial viability and rate of returns are resolved.

The river Kaladan flows from India's Mizoram to Sittwe through Myanmarese part of Chin state. Kaladan River is the biggest waterway in the locality. The coastal region in western Myanmar is separated from the mainland by the Rakhine Yoma mountain range. The Sittwe Port, at the mouth of the Kaladan River in Rakhine coast is an important harbour, which emerged as a center for rice export after British occupation in 1826 (Berlin). Earlier it was a small village of fishing communities and farmers.

During the visit of India's External Affairs Minister Pranab Mukherjee to Myanmar in April 2008, he met the Prime Minister Gen Soe Win, the Planning and Economic Development Minister U Soe Tha and his counterpart U Nyan. There he had elaborate discussions on the Kaladan project (The Hindu, 2008). Earlier, a meeting between the high ranking officials from Light Infantry Battalion of Myanmar and the engineers from Mizoram was organized in Lawng Tlai, a border town where many issues related to the development of the water way to Mizoram were discussed. Meanwhile, a delegation of Mizoram government officials met Prime Minister Dr Manmohan Sigh in New Delhi to discuss on the project. The meeting, held in the Prime Minister's office on 19 January, 2008 studied the detailed project report prepared by RITES in presence of high-level officials of the Union government (economictimes.indiatimes.com).

India's move to invest in a Myanmarese port assumes strategic significance as Bangladesh is not willing to give India access to Chittagong port, which is closer to North-East. Moreover, the Bangladesh government has been showing unwillingness to provide space to run a gas pipeline from Myanmar to mainland India through its territory. Besides, New Delhi again wants to engage the traditional regime of Myanmar in greater economic exercise with an aim to prevent Chinese potential clout in Muanmar (Sharma, 2008).

Strategically, both of the regional powers, India and China, want exactly the same thing from Burma. China wants access to ports in Burma for entry point to Indian Ocean. India wants the right to use the rivers and sea-ports in Burma for while, providing sea-access to land-locked North-Eastern States of India (Egreteau, Renaud, 2003). How far the regime of Myanmar is willing to balance the two is difficult to predict. So far China has had an edge over India in Myanmar. Due to this consideration India tried to engage with the military junta even though the pro-democracy movement in Myanmer was in pick.

Asian Highway Project

The Asian Highway project is a joint project among countries in Asia and the United Nations Economic and Social Commission for Asia and the Pacific (ESCAP) to advance the highway systems in Asia. It is one of the three aspects of Asian Land Transport Infrastructure Development project, endorsed by the ESCAP commission at its forty-eighth session

Source: www.bharat-rakshak.com

in 1992, comprising Asian Highway, Trans-Asian Railway and facilitation of land transport projects. The project was initiated by the United Nations in 1959 with the aim of promoting the development of international road transport in the region (UN ESCAP, 2004). During the first phase of the project considerable progress was achieved. However, progress slowed down when financial assistance was suspended during seventies.

The Intergovernmental Agreement on the Asian Highway Network was adopted on 18 November, 2003, by the Intergovernmental Meeting of United Nations Economic and Social Commission for Asia and the Pacific (ESCAP).The Intergovernmental Agreement includes Annex I, which identifies 55 Asian Highway routes among 32 member countries and Annex II deals with the Design Standards. During the 60th session of the ESCAP Commission at Shanghai, China, in April 2004, the Agreement was finally signed by 23 countries.(www.e-pao.net).

The ambitious project of Asian Highway 1 is proposed to extend from Tokyo to the border with Bulgaria west of Istanbul and Edirne, passing through Korea, China and other countries in Southeast, Central and South Asia. The corridor is expected to improve trade links between East Asian countries, India and Russia. To complete the route, existing roads are to be upgraded and new roads constructed to link the network. US$ 25 billion has been spent as of 2007 and additional US$ 18 billion is needed for and improvements and upgradation for the 26,000 km of the highway. This project can succeed only with domestic stability within these countries is achieved. Peace and stability is the first requirement for regional integration.

India has been an active member of the Asian Highway project since its inception. A number of road engineers from India have participated in Japanese-financed training activities conducted by ESCAP. As one of the largest countries in Asia, both in terms of land area and population, India depends heavily on its road network for transporting domestic freight, including daily necessities. With economic growth improved road connectivity has become essential so that all states within the Indian union are able to benefit from upgrowing economic growth. Traffic is increasing and so is the need for new construction and improved maintenance of roads. Thus, the Government of India is mobilizing resources through such means as road development funds, and is developing a legal framework for the introduction of build-operate-transfer (BOT) schemes (www.sinlung.com).

The progress made so far on the Asian Highway provides a solid basis for its further development. The new agreement between the Bangladesh-India-Myanmar-Sri Lanka-Thailand Economic Cooperation (BIMST-EC) members to further develop the Asian Highway connections between their countries is one example of the potential of this project for strong and lasting regional cooperation (Mayumi, Inoue and Hazarika, 2005).

Cross-border Issues

Apprehensions are also there highlighting the possible threat to both human development and national security that may arise out of the whole process of integration. A pessimist view appears to see North-East as a gateway to twin pillars of drug trafficking and cross-border terrorism. North-East's close proximity to Myanmar enhances this threat as latter is considered as second largest opium producing countries in the world and is operational base for many of the terrorist outfits of the North-Eastern states. It is also connected to the Islamist terrorist hub of Southeast Asia. Thus opening of trade roots may give access to international terrorism to enter into the Indian soil.

(a) Drug trafficking

Drugs, HIV/AIDS, violence, conflict, wide spread poverty, underdevelopment are some of the major characteristics of India's troubled north-east region. Assam, Meghalaya, Sikkim, Tripura, Arunachal Pradesh, Mizuram,

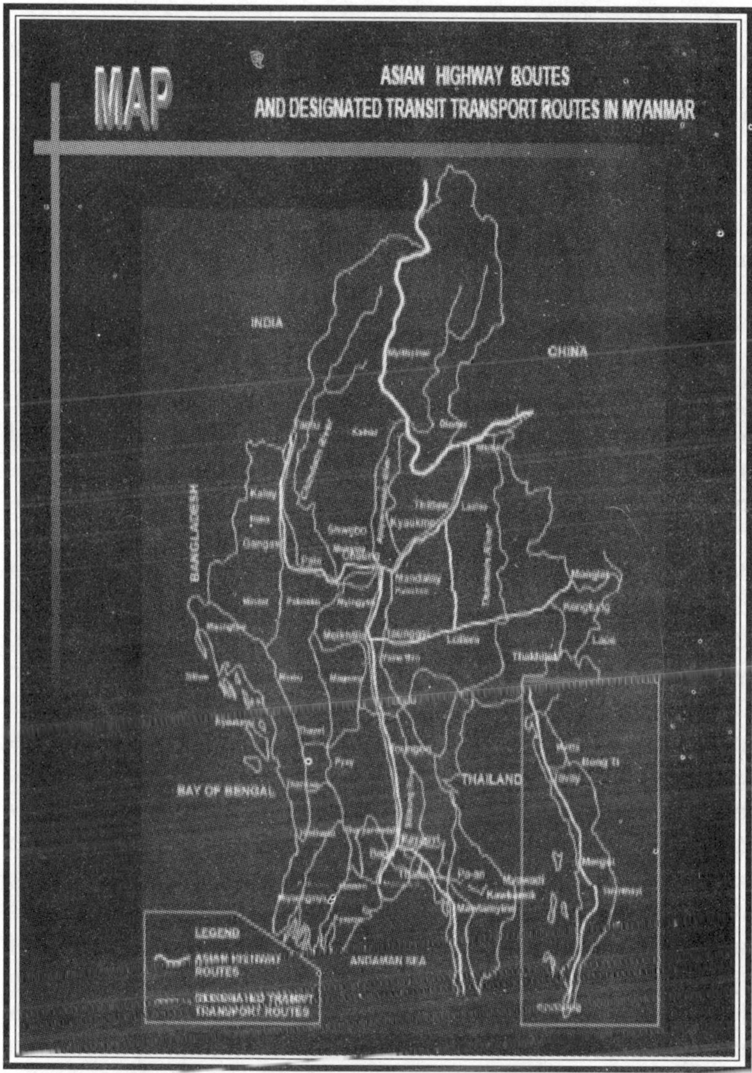

Source: www.iorier.org

and Nagaland are the eight states of this region and last four share a common international border with Myanmar which is as stated earlier, considered as the world's second largest illicit opium producing country. Following the introduction of heroin in 1970s, drug use among the local youth in the region, particularly states close to Myanmar, created a new problem in the region. Many people, in their teen age started drug use (Lama, 2001). Wide range of structural and environmental factors, including underdevelopment, increased the vulnerability of the young people to drug use. Easy availability of drugs, stress arising from socio-political unrest and frustration out of lack of employment opportunities are often cited as the major causes of drug use (www.unodc.org)

India's troubled Northeast is situated on the western corner of Burma's infamous "Golden Triangle". The International Narcotics Control Bureau (INCB), in a global report, has said that more than 70 per cent of the amphetamines available worldwide are produced in countries around the Golden Triangle, particularly Burma. The INCB report ranks Burma as second to Afghanistan in opium production. Between 1985 and 1995, Burma's heroin output rose from 54 tones to 166 tones. What is more worrying about the 'Golden Triangle' is the eight-times rise in the production of amphetamines from an estimated 100 million tablets in 1993 to 800 million tablets in 2002 (www.gluckman.com/BurmaBorder). Amphetamines are cheap and popular as performance-enhancing drugs, as much in demand in Calcutta or Delhi as in London or New York (Bhaumik, 2005). Drug trafficking across the common border of Myanmar and the eastern most three states of India, Manipur, Mizuram and Nagaland has gone up to a serious level. It is only from Myanmar alone 20 million rupees of drugs are supplied to the North-East region per month. The drug mafias enter Assam and other parts of North-East India through More region in Manipur and Champhai region in Mizuram. In the January month of 2007, the Border Security Force raided 75.25 lakhs of narcotic drugs in the Indo-Myanmar border. Most significantly a major section of the students' community has become involved with this drug trade. According to the estimates by the National Aids Control Organization (NACO, 2005, www.naco.org), there are 50,000

IDU injecting drug uses in the region and majority of them are in Manipur, Nagaland, Mizuram, Meghalaya.

In January 2002, the six countries – Thailand, Myanmar, Laos, Cambodia, Vietnam and China – set up the 'Joint Special Task Unit 2002' to coordinate the fight against drug trafficking. India is yet to join this initiative, despite clear indications that Burmese drug cartels are increasingly using Northeast Indian states to send their deadly cargo into Bangladesh, mainland India or Nepal and to other regional and global markets. The region's drug addict population is currently estimated at around 1, 20,000 by the Indian Council of Medical Research (ICMR). Many addicts use intravenous injections to push drugs and become HIV positive. North-East India ranks second in HIV prone areas in India (Hazra, 2002).

Several military and paramilitary officials have been arrested for smuggling heroin and lesser drugs in North-East. Sridharn, (2004) mentions that the drug lobby has made good relation with the several politicians, bureaucrats and even security force officials to carry on their illicit trade. Unless checked firmly, this trend is dangerous for the morale of Indian security forces

Ethnic separatists in India's North-East have been protecting the drug mafias and use them as means to raise funds. Some like the Manipur Peoples Liberation Front continue to fiercely resist the drug traffickers, but other groups, including the NSCN, have entered into the drug trade.

(b) Terrorism

India's North-East is one of South Asia's hottest trouble spots, not simply because the region has as many as 30 armed insurgent organizations operating and fighting the Indian state, but because trans-border linkages that these groups have, and strategic alliances among them, have acted as force multipliers and have made the conflict dynamics all the more intricate. With demands of these insurgent groups ranging from secession to autonomy and the right to self-determination, and a plethora of ethnic groups clamouring for special rights and the protection of their distinct identity, the region is bound to be a turbulent one (Kamboj, 2006).

Moreover, the location of the eight northeastern Indian States itself is part of the reason why it has always been a hotbed of militancy with trans-border ramifications. This region of 2,63,000 square kilometers shares highly porous and sensitive frontiers with China in the North, Myanmar in the East, Bangladesh in the South West and Bhutan to the North West. The region's strategic location is underlined by the fact that it shares a 4,500 km-long international border with its four South Asian neighbours, but is connected to the Indian mainland by a tenuous 22 km-long land corridor passing through Siliguri in the eastern State of West Bengal, appropriately described as the 'Chicken's Neck.' (Gopalakrishnan, 1991).

The 'rebel factor' has emerged as one of the most significant issues in India-Burma relations. In the early 1950s, the Naga National Council (NNC) in India's Naga Hills came into contact with the Eastern Naga Regional Council (ENRC) that was active in Burma's Sagaing region which has some Naga-inhabited areas (Banerjee, 1997). The ENRC joined the NNC in propounding the concept of a 'Greater Naga Nation' in which Nagas of India and Burma would live together. The ENRC provided the NNC the first links to the Kachin Independence Army (KIA) and helped the Naga Army fighters to reach China. As the Indian Army tightened its grip in the Naga Hills and East Pakistan was lost as a safe base area in 1971, the NNC turned to Burma's Sagaing region to set up some major bases (Singh, 2007).

When the NNC disintegrated after the 1975 Shillong Accord, its breakaway faction, the National Socialist Council of Nagaland (NSCN) shifted its main headquarters to the remote Tepak Mountains in Sagaing division. With S.S. Khaplang as their Vice-President, the NSCN was firmly entrenched amongst the Hemi Nagas of western Burma. Manipuri rebels as well as the United Liberation Front of

Assam (ULFA) had also set up bases around the NSCN headquarters. In 1985-86, these rebels faced two Burmese military offensives but managed to beat them back (Roy, 2005).

The Manipuri National Front (MNF) maintained a large number of bases in Burma's Chin Hills, further south of Sagaing, though their main headquarters were located in Bangladesh's Chittagong Hill Tracts (Kotwal, D, 2000). These bases were dismantled when the MNF signed an accord with the Indian government in 1986. But over the years, the Northeast Indian rebel presence in Burma has increased. Now, the NSCN (Khaplang faction), the ULFA and the Manipuri rebel groups maintain at least 27 camps in Burmese territory. The NSCN's Muivah faction pulled out of Burma after the spat with Khaplang that led to the split in the NSCN in 1988. While Khaplang's fighters are based in the wild Tepak Mountains inside Sagaing division, the ULFA has few bases close to the Indian border. The Manipur Peoples Liberation Front (MPLF), a coalition of three leading Meitei rebel groups, has a number of bases around the town of Tamu and close to Molcham salient, while their main base in Manipur's Sajit Tampak area is located right on the border with Burma (Baruah, 2002).

In November 2001, the Burmese army raided four Manipuri rebel bases, rounded up 192 rebels and seized more than 1600 weapons. Surprisingly, the Burmese later released these rebels including UNLF chief Rajkumar Meghen. While the Burmese junta claims that they attacked Khaplang's base area in December 2004 and killed nearly 100 rebel fighters, they did not seized the Meitei insurgent's bases in 2001. The Naga bases are located in much more difficult terrain than those of the Manipuri groups or the ULFA. It could well be that the Nagas are Burmese nationals and their demand to be a part of Greater Naga state is seen as a threat to Burmese sovereignty by the military junta (Kamboj, 2006).

With India's relations improved with Burma in the mid-nineties, the Burmese army participated in a joint operation called 'Golden Bird' in April-May 1995. The 57 Indian Mountain Division was blocking a large rebel column of more than 200 NSCN, ULFA and Manipuri fighters who had picked up a huge consignment of weapons south of Cox's Bazar on the Bangladesh coast, from moving through the Mizoram-Burma border towards Manipur (Datta, 2000). With India awarding the Nehru Peace Prize to Aung Sang Suu Kyi, the military junta pulled out of the joint operation, allowing the trapped rebel column to escape.

In the recent past, the military-to-military relations between India and Burma improved dramatically. Myanmar's military chief, General Maung Aye visited India twice, once to meet the regional commanders at Shillong and then to meet his counterpart in Delhi. During Maung Aye's second visit to Delhi, India and Myanmar signed an agreement for 'increased cooperation to tackle cross-border terrorism and drugs trafficking. India's relation with Myanmar has got new boost with the then India President Dr. A.P.J abdul Kalam visit to Myanmar in 2006. Considering such security and strategic reason New Delhi maintained a very diplomatic stand during the India's engagement with pro-democracy protest by the monks in Myanmar (Parthasarthy, 2008).

These are some of the challenges that Indian policy makers have to deal with. The fear that connectivity could give access to the drug mafias and cross border terrorist elements to make their entry to India is the adverse side of opening border roads. But potentials in this regard can't be undermined. That is why India is slow in implementing some of the schemes. After all national security has to be considered.

4

Prospects for Development and Issues Involved

Introduction

North-East India, the land-locked region of India with its poor infrastructure, could not so far develop its industry and trade beyond its traditional areas of oil, tea, paper, coal etc. The location of the region which is far away from markets is one of the major reasons of industrial backwardness. The region shares longest international border stretching over 5000 km. with five foreign countries and this is being utilized for opening trade with the neighbouring countries.

Initiatives to improve cross-border trade with Myanmar have resulted in a declaration of Free Trade Zone at Moreh, the international border point in Manipur, in 1994. It is stated it would help improve the socio economic conditions of Manipur and the entire region.

In 2003, during his China visit, then Prime Minister Atal Behari Vajpayee floated the idea of reopening the trade routes to Southeast Asia and linking North-East India with Asian neighbourhood (www. india nembassy.org/policy/foreign_policy/2004/2004).This idea got consolidated into the "Look-East Policy". The present UPA government is also keenly translating this policy as fast as possible into reality, but within the parameter of regional environment. The

Confederation of Indian Industries (CII), took an initiative and led a delegation to Myanmar with an effort to open the gateway to the Southeast Asian market. The visit of Thailand's commerce minister along with the country's biggest trade and investment agencies to India's North-Eastern region in April 2008 has boosted its faster trade prospects.

The Ministry of Development of the North-East Region (DoNER) as well as the state governments has invited investors to take business advantages offered by the region's tremendous commercial and profitable investment projects. The investment advantages and fiscal concessions offered by the North-East Industrial and Investment Promotion Policy 2007 have virtually turned the whole region into a special economic zone (SEZ). The subsequent North-East Business Summits have brought about an impressive response from prospective investors.

India has signed an agreement to established free trade with Thailand at Bangkok in October, 2003. It covers 82 items for exchange of concessions coverage between the two countries and was implemented in September, 2004. The trade negotiation committee is now in the process of working out a free trade agreement (FTA) in goods, services and investment. Apart from the Bay of Bengal initiative for Multi-sectoral Technical and Economic Co-operation (BIMSTEC), Free Trade Area was singed in February, 2004 among India, Bangladesh, Bhutan, Myanmar, Nepal, Sri Lanka, and Thailand.

The North-East region has immense potential. Efforts must be directed to tap its resources to give a fillip to trade with our neighbouring countries. Efforts for the possible development of infrastructure of the region must be made along with opening of avenues of trade.

Economic Developments for North-East India in Look-East Policy

The Look-East policy has tried to promote commercial links between North-Eastern states and the neighbouring countries to try and break the economic and geographic isolation of this region from the rest of the country. The North East region has a 37 km. link with India, but 4500 km. of border with the newly emerging nations of Asia, say China, Burma (Myanmar), Bangladesh, Bhutan, and Nepal. All products consumed in the North East came to be imported from distant manufacturing regions in India. It is hardly surprising that with closed borders and open ports, the North East is not part of India's trade expansion strategy with eastern neighbours (Baruah 2004).Though the North-East has enormous natural and human resources, it has always been neglected.

In the context of "Look-East" policy, North-East has been seen with a new vigour and vitality. Rajiv Sikri, Secretary East, Ministry of External Affairs, mentions that the Look East Policy "envisages the NE region not as the periphery of India, but as the centre of a thriving and integrated economic space linking two dynamic regions with a network of highways, railways, pipelines, transmission lines crisscrossing the region"(Baruah, 2005).Advocates of free trade visualize the region getting maximum benefit from this economic policy which will bring economic prosperity in North-East.

In the light of the existing impact of this policy, we need to investigate whether the policy is going to benefit the region? If yes, how far? And, who will be the real beneficiaries of the cross border trade, is it the people of the region or the business community of mainland India?

The "Look-East" policy seems to indicate a strategic in dimension with India looking beyond South Asia. It has been more than two decade since the policy was launched, now it is the time to discuss the impact of this on what it has set out to achieve. It is a fact that economic growth and development of a region depends on trade and business with other regions, the crucial question is where does North-East India stand in the India-ASEAN trade relations? (NE Vision 2020)

In the light of the ongoing "Look-East policy" process, North-East India serves the function of a gateway indicating that trade will take place between mainland India and the members of ASEAN. The region will perform the role of a consumer and buyer rather than that of a producer and seller. Goods consumed by the people of the region are all made either in China or Thailand. Local markets are flooded with manufactured goods, and agricultural commodities. India's exports consist mainly cement, cycles, drugs and pharmaceuticals, auto parts and cotton yarn, which are manufactured and produced in the advanced mainland Indian States. In this sense, the Indo-Myanmar border trade can be held to be an expansion of both the trading partner's market in the North-East region. From this expansion of market, people of the region may have the opportunity of readily available final goods. But this will have an adverse affects on the economy as well. The immediate effect is that since they only buy and do not sell, money will go out from the region. This forfeits the chance of a self sufficient and prosperous economy in the region in the future, thus paving the way for an entirely dependent economy. Another important question is who are the business people that have been actively taking part in this trade? If this business community is not the residents of the State, then their main intention would be to make money rather contributing towards the welfare of the region (Baruah, 2005)

There are some experts who feel that New Delhi's "Look-East policy" strategy may by-pass North-East region in this India-ASEAN trade, due to shaky infrastructure facilities and stagnant economic environment of the region. They see the region not ready for border trade. In terms of both peoples' involvement and export of goods, the region is not taking part in this border trade. So, if the policy is to benefit the region economically in order to bring development in the true sense then the, main emphasize has to be placed in developing indigenous industries in the region, such as textile, handicraft, bamboo industry etc and improve infrastructure with greater involvement of the local people.

Prospective Areas

(a) Tourism

The North-East India has huge tourism potential, but it has not been fully exploited. The Ministry of Tourism calls the region a 'paradise unexplored'. It has been noticed that global tourism has been booming and future projections show that this trend will continue. For these new and growing breed of tourists the North-East with its variety and uniqueness holds immense attraction. The rich natural beauty and its diversity, striking cultural and ethnic variety, flora and fauna, unexplored ecosystems provide possibilities of a totally different experience for the tourists (Bhattacharya, 1996).

The rationale for a trade led growth strategy for the North-East integrated to the 'Look-East policy' has been well explained. The landlocked North-East, it is explained, is ideally placed to link India with ASEAN both in a geographical and commercial sense. The Northeast also has strong cultural and historical linkages with the East, which could be exploited to enhance economic cooperation. The marketing strategy of the Ministry of Tourism is now identifying new markets for tourism and this search is aligned with the Look East trade policy (The Hindu, 2007). Such a policy is particularly relevant and important for the North-East, as it is situated far away from the main entry points of tourists, the North-East is at a disadvantage in attracting foreign tourists from the West and this is reflected in the negligible tourist flow to this region. In 2002, out of about 5.8 million tourist visiting India, the North-East received only about 22000 (www.india-seminar.com/2005/550/550%20m).

Looking to the East is a natural marketing option for the North East. It is projected that by 2020 the Asia Pacific region will be the second largest tourist generating market in the world. The world tourism projection shows that by 2020 this region will generate 405 m of the total 1561 m tourists. These countries have continuous geographical land links with the North-East (www.articlenotes.com). China is already energetically developing tourism in its southern provinces to take advantage of this outbound tourist market of the region. These areas have cultural, historical and ethnic links with the India's North-East region. The tourism promotion strategy of the North-East should focus on these links to establish a natural flow of people to the region.

In such a strategy it will be of crucial importance to build access to this region. In the present scenario, access to the Northeast is seen as a constraint. While air access will have to be developed as an important tourism development strategy, the Asian Highway Project will bring great opportunity for the region. The Asian Highway, if properly planned and executed, can completely change the tourism picture of the region.

Moreover, tourism rectories apart requires social and economic infrastructure for proper growth. As a first step to planning, priority must be given to the infrastructure. Except Assam, the rest of the states in the North-East region are hardly having proper communication infrastructure with proper air links. The centre is not only to provide facilities but also to develop outlets for local handicraft and handloom products and showpiece local culture, cuisine etc. Such involvement leads not only to better economic benefits for the people, but also ensures better visitor experience.

Unfortunately, in spite of comparative advantage, tourism is not perceived as an important economic activity. The first task of the governments should be to create awareness about the place of tourism in general and of sustainable tourism in particular, in the socio-economic planning of the region. Civil society can play an effective role in this regard. Human resource development, creating institutional arrangements for people's participation, looking at ways to exploit greater resources for tourism, creating public-private partnerships are some of the issues which will demand attention as tourism grows.

(b) Power Sector

With India maintaining a strong growth momentum with 7.8 per cent GDP growth in the Tenth five year plan and continues to grow at an impressive level despite the high rate of inflation, the demand for power is certain to grow. It has become important to have power sector reforms emphasizing of establishment of thermal – hydel and non-conventional energy supply sources with the involvement of private sector investment.

Assam, Arunachal Pradesh, Manipur, Mizoram, Meghalaya, Nagaland and Tripura, have reservoir of rich natural resources. Since the region is a prospective hub of international trade and business, power sector may emerge as a potential area of investment with the growing linkage of India and ASEAN. The region offers immense investment opportunity in the hydel power sector. More than two-third of the country's hydropower potential exits in the North-East region (The Hindu, 2007). According to the estimates of the North-Eastern Power Corporation (NEEPCO), the region has the potential of about 60,000 MW, but out of this only about two per cent has been tapped so far. States like Arunachal Pradesh. Sikkim, Meghalaya, have substantial hydro-power potential which has largely remained untapped (www.neepco.com). The region has a reserve of 151.68 billion cubic feet natural gas and 864.78 million tones of coal. Investments in the power sector in the region would not only facilitate the socio- economic growth and development in the entire region, but also supply power to other Indian states which will help them partially to meet their energy requirements. But, in spite of such huge potential, the region ranks lowest in the country in terms of power generation and per capita energy consumption. It is mainly because of the lack of proper planning and its remoteness. There is also an imbalance between hydel power and thermal power generation. The transmission and distribution sector is weak in the North-East India which in consequence has resulted in huge losses.

Among the North-Eastern States Arunachal Pradesh has the highest hydro-electrical potential. With estimated 27000 MW it ranks first in the country in terms of hydro-electrical power potential. The state has 37 power plants ranging from 5 KW to 4500 KW with total installed capacity of 405 MW. Some of its major hydroelectrical plants are Ranganadi Hydro Power project, Kameng Hydro Power project, Siang Hydro Power project etc.

Assam too has enormous potential for electrical power generation. But even then the power sector has not made much progress. The state purchases power from other sources to meet its domestic needs. The Assam State Electricity Board (ASEB) has six installed projects with total installed capacity of 574 MW. The major power generating plants in Assam include Borguli Thermal Power plant, Karbi Langpi Thermal Power plant, Amguri Gas based project, Kathalguri Gas based project etc.

The state of Manipur has two small hydro projects and twenty- two diesel projects with total installed capacity of about 10 MW. Loktak hydro-electrical project is a central sector project in Manipur.

Meghalaya is rich in thermal power potential. It has vast coal reserve with high sulphur content which is appropriate for setting up thermal power projects. Meghalaya has a total installed capacity of 185.20 MW. The state government and the North Eastern Council have taken several steps to develop thermal as well as hydro power generating stations in the state.

In spite of its huge hydro electrical potential, Mizoram has not been able to exploit its resources. It has 22 isolated diesel power stations and 9 small stations with installed capacity of 26.14 MW. To fill the big gap between the demand and supply, the state has to buy power from outside sources.

The state of Nagaland is capable of generating only 4.26 MW of power against the requirement of 42 MW. This huge demand-supply imbalance makes the state to purchase power from centrally owned power projects like NHPC and

NEEPCO. The state has taken up a thermal power station in Dimapur with 24 MW power generation capacities.

Sikkim too has huge power potential, especially hydro power. It has total 37.70 MW installed capacity and can play an important role in transnational energy diplomacy.

Tripura is also not balanced power generation state. It has five state owned installed projects. NEEPCO has commissioned a 84 MW Gas Turbine project in Agartala.

It is expected that the government's growing focus on the "Look-East Policy" will help in exploiting the full potential of the hydro- power sector in the North-Eastern region (Verghese, 2005). As per the demand estimate, the region requires modernization of the exiting energy facilities in order to cope with the growing power demand for economic growth and industrialization. It needs private sector involvement in the region. Public-Private Partnership (PPP) would be the most effective measure in tapping the power potentiality of the region. The FDI from the ASEAN countries like Singapore, Malaysia, and Thailand would prove to be effective in the power generation process. Since FDI up to 100 per cent is allowed in India for projects related to the electricity generation, transmission and distribution, the foreign companies, particularly those from Southeast Asia must look at the huge opportunities that exit in the power sector in the North-East India with great interest. The already negotiated India-Thailand FTA and India-ASEAN FTA have the potential of improving the power scenario in region. Comprehensive Economic Cooperation Agreement (CECA) with Singapore is another important dimension.

The possibility of energy trading among the Southeast Asian countries and the North-East India has opened new doors of cooperation. It has been seen that economic growth in the East and Southeast Asian countries has increased energy requirements. India can get benefit from this growing demand for energy with its unexploited huge potentials of power generation in the North-Eastern region. In this sense the region can play a pivotal role in the context of regional energy integration (Himal Southasian, 2007). The proposed India-Bangladesh- Myanmar gas pipe line is in deadlocked mode due to number of reasons. One of the major reasons is lack of good will on the part Bangladesh. As per the negotiation India has to pay $125 million transit fees to Bangladesh. Again Bangladesh is also asking for transport corridor via India to Nepal. The government of India can change the direction of the pipeline by make its entry into India through its North-East region rather trying via Bangladesh. In this context the North-East India will not only minimize the negative factors associated with the pipeline also make it cost effective.

Table 4.1: Power Installed Capacity of the States in the North-Eastern Region in MW as on 2006, Estimated by NEEPCO

States	Hydro	Thermal	Renewable	Total
Assam	333	797.7	0.2	1130.9
Arunachal Pradesh	116.5	36.9	26	179.4
Meghalaya	258.6	28.1	1.5	288.2
Tripura	87	165.3	1.1	244.5
Manipur	82.5	71.4	4	157.9
Nagaland	78.5	21	3.2	102.7
Mizoram	38	67.9	10	116.8
Sikkim	40	67	9.1	116.1
Total	1153.1	1311.2	56	2520.3

Source: www.neepco.com

(c) Indigenous Industrial Development

Assam is the only North-Eastern state having a reasonably good industrial base. Major industries of Assam are tea, plywood, crude oil and natural gas, coal, paper, petrochemicals, fertilisers and textiles (Baruah and Srinath, 1999). Assam accounts for more than 50 per cent of tea

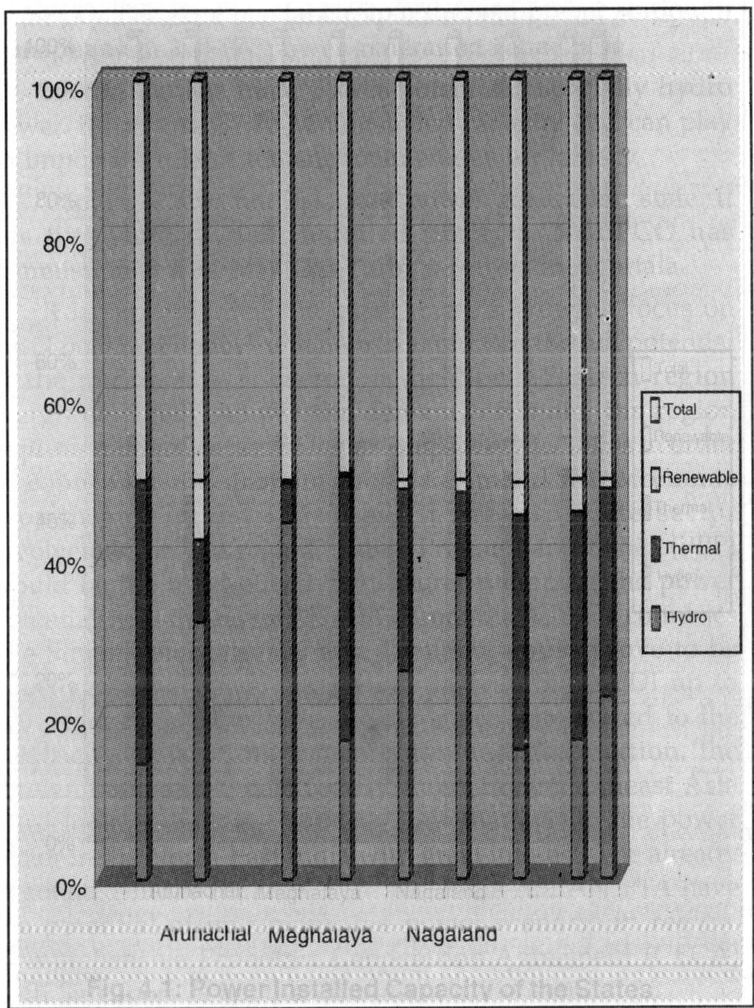

Fig. 4.1: Power Installed Capacity of the States

produced in the country. The state produces a variety of fruits including pineapple, banana, oranges and papaya. Sericulture is a traditional industry of Assam. Eri, Muga and Mulberry are special types of silk produced in the state. Muga, in fact, is the monopoly of the state. Plywood and safety match industries are the major forest based industries. Forest area covering 22 per cent of the total land area of Assam contributes substantially to the state's revenue. Handmade paper industry and cane and bamboo industry are the other industries at small and cottage level. Besides, there are more than 300 varieties of medicinal plants and herbs grown in the forests of Assam. Assam has rich resources of coal, limestone, china clay, sillimanite, granite, barlys and gypsum apart from its oil and gas reserves. The Assam Industrial Development Corporation has identified potential areas for investment. These are hydro electric power, coal based industries, food processing, floriculture, inland fishery, granite mining and polishing as export oriented industries and infrastructure projects.

The state of Tripura has an international border running into 839 kms. with Bangladesh. Its economy is agrarian, with paddy as its main agricultural crop. Other agricultural crops are pulses, oilseeds and jute. Some horticultural products including oranges, pineapples, bananas, lemons and arecanuts are also grown in the state. Natural rubber has emerged as an important plantation product in the state. The state also produces a substantial quantity of tea annually. Bamboo based handicraft industry is one of the main economic activities of the state. Natural rubber products like tyres, tubes and gloves, various processed food items, handmade paper and packing materials are some other potential areas (Sachdeva, G, 1999)

Meghalaya has rich mineral resources such as coal, limestone, clay and sillimanite. Coal and limestone are being exported to Bangladesh through its border. Rich uranium deposits are also found in the state, which await exploitation.

The industries that are operating in Manipur are cycles and cycle parts, cement, pulp and paper products, vanaspati oil, drugs and pharmaceuticals, steel and iron rods, spinning and weaving mills, plastic and plastic products, fruit processing, soap and toiletry products, rubber and rubber products, disposable syringes, hosiery and hosiery products, mineral based industrial products and television sets, both colour and black and white.

Mizoram is predominantly an agricultural economy. The state has rich forest resources including cane and bamboo. The state has mineral resources which have yet to be exploited.

Major occupation of Nagaland is paddy cultivation. A large number of items including engineering products, textiles, plastic items, food products, toileteries, electrical and electronics can be developed in the state. In addition, the state has a number of sericulture farms, reeling and spinning units and cocoon preservation centres. Besides, industrial establishments for food processing can be set up, utilising local production of items like guava, pineapple, bananas, oranges and tomatoes (Kumar and De Prabir, 2004).

Local Industrial Export Prospects with ASEAN Countries

Local food processing industries are not much developed in Myanmar. This advantage can be taken by the states such as Assam, Tripura and Manipur with creating facilities for processed fruits and vegetables like orange, lemon, jackfruit, ginger, papaya, banana, potato, chilly pineapple etc. Assam has tremendous scope for tea packaging and blending industry (Goswami and Gogoi, 2005)

Myanmar provides import scope for tyres and tubes for heavy duty vehicles. Other rubber products are under the import items list. Tripura can effectively utilize this opportunity as RMAI rubber is available in the state. If power supply is ensured cycle tyres and tubes can be manufactured for exports.

Myanmar's forest area near the Indo-Myanmar border has abundant growth of teak. High transportant costs to Yangon and Mandalay prohibit the timber to be taken for processing to those centres. This disadvantage can be exploited by India by setting up processing centres at Moreh, Chambhai and Lungwa. There is substantial demand for stainless steel utensils in Myanmar. As there is no local production, demand is met by imports, especially from Thailand. Production units can be set up at Moreh to make stainless steel and aluminium utensils for exports to Myanmar. Another industry which has much potential of growth is bamboo industry. North-Eastern states are having abundance of bamboos. These productions can be commercially utilized for export (Sachdeva, 2000).

Border Trade with Myanmar

The governments of India and Myanmar signed a Border Trade Agreement on 21 January, 1994 with the goal of formalization of border trade practices. The agreement initially provided for cross border trade in twenty two products, mostly agricultural and primary commodities. In 2001 a few items were added to the list of tradable items. The agreement specified that trade should be conducted through the designated customs posts, viz, Moreh in Manipur and Tamu in Myanmar, Champhai in Mizoram and Hri in Myanmar and some other places may be notified by mutual agreement between the two countries. Following the signing of the agreement the two land custom stations at Moreh and Champhai in India were notified. However, the Champhai station has not become functional till date and all the formal Indo- Myanmar border trade has been taking place through the Moreh-Tamu route (Indian Institute of Foreign Trade, 1998)

Soon after the formal border trade agreement, there was growth in formal trade across the Moreh-Tamu sector. Starting from about Rs. 15 crores in 1995-96, the trade volume reached almost Rs. 47 croces in 1996-97. But even after such improvement, in the total volume of India- Myanmar international trade, formal border trade across the North-East is virtually negligible. For instance, in 2002-03 formal border trades across the North-East constituted only 1.05 per cent of India's export, and 0.71 per cent of import. The recent data shows that the amount of formal border trade has got dramatically reduced. In the volume of export from India, the share of wheat has drastically come down from 76 per cent to 10 per cent. The decline in imports through formal route is even more pathetic. Imports are now restricted only to one commodity, that is betel nut (Yumnam, 1999)

One of the main reasons for such decline of the formal border trade is the exiting rigidness in the trading agreements. The Agreement of 1994 limits the items to be traded across the border and the free flow of trade. Since as per the arrangement, trade transactions are to be recorded in hard currencies, gross over- valuation of Myanmar' currency as per their official exchange rates discourages trade to flow through the formal channels. The official exchange rate Kyat is rated at Rupees 7 whereas according to one survey, the ongoing exchange rate is Kyat 20 to 21 for a Rupee at the Moreh-Tamu sector and Kyat 18 for a Rupee at the Champhai-Hri sector. These markets determined informal rates make trades to choose more informal border trade across the India-Myanmar border. With putting in place a legitimate system of transit trade and progressively cutting down of custom duties, the formal trade will expand. So the government has to emphasize on it to have benefit from the border trade with Myanmar.

Trade Potentials Between Myanmar and North-East India

Although agriculture has the larger share in domestic production of the North-East region, it is deficient in production of quite a few agricultural commodities. It is dependent on other parts of India for its requirement of pulses and rice. The supply of these items involves large transport cost. Myanmar is traditionally surplus producer of these two items. Goswami and Gogoi (2005) mentions that North-East India can provide markets for agricultural products from Myanmar. Export of such products can benefit the farm production of both Myanmar and North-East India. With the supply of such food items from Myanmar, the farmers of North-East India can be able to concentrate more on production of high value horticultural and other commercial crops.

Myanmar has various types of mineral deposits. North-East India can provide an effective market for the granites produced in Myanmar. North-East India will have transport cost advantage of importing granites from Myanmar than from states like Rajasthan and Maharastra for construction purposes. The precious stones like Jade and Ruby which are having deposits in Myanmar can also be imported through the North-East India (Verghese, 2004).

Myanmar also has a rich deposit of natural gas. Indian companies including the ONGC are already engaged in exploring and production in Myanmar. With the growing economy of India, the demand for energy is rising rapidly. Gas supply from Myanmar can be a great advantage for Indian economy. Already the government of India has taken an initiative towards laying pipelines for importing gas from Myanmar. Since laying pipelines through Bay of Bengal is likely to be far more expensive and also there are much apprehension from the side Bangladesh side, it is proposed to use the North-Eastern route.

The region has a significant capacity for refining crude oil. The four refineries located in the state of Assam can provide a substantial exportable surplus. This surplus can be exported to Myanmar. In a liberalized trading environment between the two countries refinery products like kerosene can easily get market access in Myanmar (Das, et.al., 2005). Though Chinese penetration might have reduced India's share in the market for manufactured goods in Myanmar, in certain items like medicine and fertilizers India still has substantial share. The Indian manufacturers can set up production in the North-East region for exporting to the markets of Myanmar. Considering such advantages, attractive fiscal and other concession have been provided under the North-East Industrial and Investment Promotion Policy 2007 by the government of India.

Services sector is another potential area of trade between Myanmar and North-East India. The services in health care, tourism can generate trade in transport, communication, and other prospective fields. The advance health facilities which are available in Guwahati, can be taken by the residents of Myanmar too like the other north-eastern states, if the free movement of people is allowed across the border. Tourism is another potential service from which both North-East India and Myanmar can be mutually benefited.

The prospect of trade between North-East India and Myanmar is very high. But to facilitate such prospects the government has to consider seriously the factors like poor infrastructure, rigidness in the exiting trade agreements, over-valuation of Myanmar' currency etc. A liberalized system of border trade can make North-East India and Myanmar an attractive transit route for trade and even between china and other East Asian and ASEAN countries on one side and India on the other (Das, and Purkayastha 2000).

Table 4.2: Value of Formal Exports and Imports Across Moreh-Tamu Sector

Year	Exports	Imports	Total Value
1995-96	10.45	5.39	15.84
1996-97	29.79	16.7	46.49
1997-98	25.16	37.19	62.35
1998-99	4.88	3.74	8.62
1999-00	3.31	6.52	9.83
2000-01	5.68	12.41	18.09
2001-02	1.29	8.13	9.42
2002-03	3.84	11.9	15.74
2003-04	9.45	8.85	18.3

Source: NER Datebank, httm//www.Nedfi.com

(d) The Mekong-Ganga Project

The Mekong-Ganga Cooperation was launched on November 10, 2000 in Vientiane, the capital of Laos to increase cooperation in tourism, culture and education. The signatories to this idea are India and five South-East Asian Nations namely Thailand, Vietnam, Laos, Cambodia and Myanmar. The idea was designed in the tune of new global economy keeping their native identity and character intact. The six countries also undertook to develop transportation networks

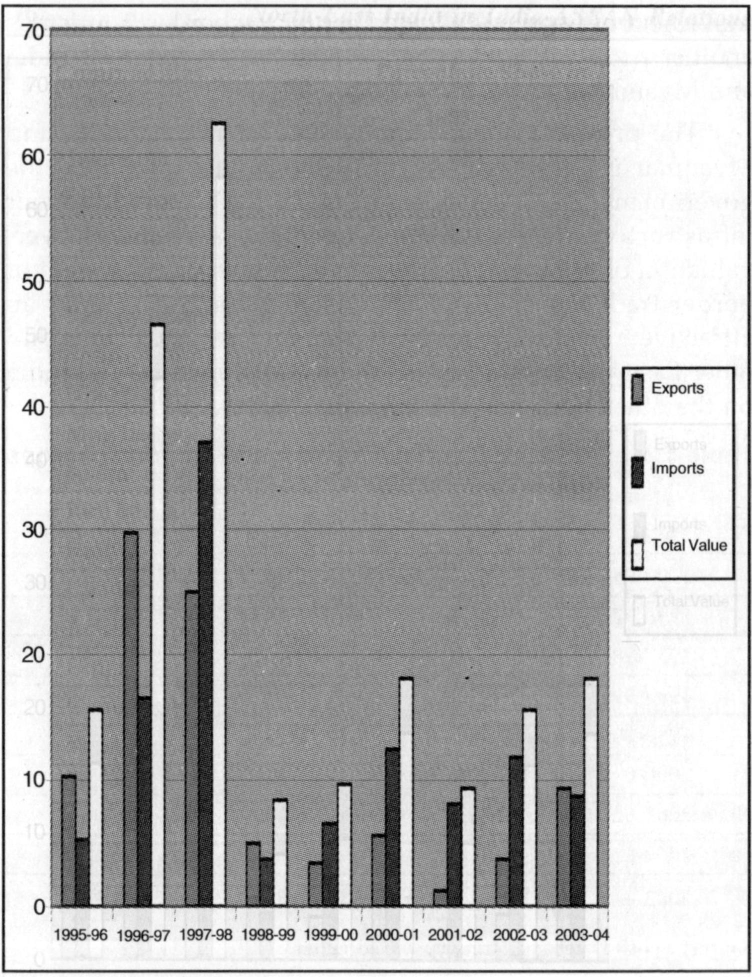

Fig. 4.2: Value of Formal Exports and Imports Across Moreh-Tamu Sector

including the East-West Corridor project and the trans-Asian highway. The ministers of India, Vietnam, Myanmar, Cambodia, Thailand and Laos signed the Vientiane Declaration, which outlines the basic theme of cooperation and made the ground for future course for rapid economic development of the Mekong region countries (Kaul, 2006).

Table 4.3: Composition of Exports Through Formal Channel

Commodities	Percentage Share in Total Value	
	1997-98	2003-04
Wheat flour	76.31	9.75
Buffalo appall		58.01
Seeds	7.49	
Rose powder	8.35	25.38
Cumin seeds	2.92	5.91
Peas	1.33	
Milk		0.95
Suger	0.28	
Stainless Steel	1.71	
Electric goods	0.41	
Hand saw	0.27	
Saw blade	0.24	
Bleaching poder	0.38	
Ammonia	0.11	
Solamonic bar	0.09	
Corriander	0.06	
Gold finger	0.04	
Common salt	0.01	
Total	100.00	100.00

Source: National Informatics Centre and NEDFi, <neidatebank@hub.nic.in

For India, the Mekong-Ganga Cooperation (MGC) offers enormous scope for creating the linkages. But one thing is very clear that without the development of the North-Eastern States, cooperation with South-East Asia cannot be meaningful. The North-East India is a crucial factor for the Mekong-Ganga Cooperation to be effective (Baruah, 2004).

Table 4.4: Composition of Imports Through Formal Channel

Commodities	Percentage Share in Total Value	
	1997-98	2003-04
Betel nuts	65.67	99.24
Chick peas	8.77	
Turmeric	6.31	
Mustard seeds	4.82	
Kidney beans	4.15	
Resin	1.8	
Urad pulse	2.71	
Mug beans	1.59	
Katha	1.15	0.07
Rice beans	0.72	
Kuth	0.6	
Chana	0.39	
Achar	0.69	
Ginger	0.21	0.68
Cumin seeds	0.16	
Reed broom	0.12	
Serpentine roots	0.08	0.01
Dry cagor	0.04	
Nimosa peedica	0.02	
Total	100.00	100.00

Source: National Informatics Centre and NEDFi, <neidatebank@hub.nic.in

If there exists sufficient trade and industry in this region, overland trade via Myanmar to many MGC countries will become a valuable proposition for India. So, New Delhi should keep in mind this crucial importance and try for infrastructural development in its North-East frontier. The Mekong-Ganga Cooperation will bring tremendous tourism prospects for the Brahmaputra valley. The starting of the Guwahati-Bangkok flight was a welcome step in this connection. But it's unfortunate that the civil aviation department could not understand its long term benefits and dropped this flight. Recently New Delhi has understood geo-strategic importance of the North-Eastern region and by exploiting the historically driven natural connectivity, it has added powerful cultural dimension to its economic diplomacy by encouraging business contacts between the people residing on the banks of Mekong and Ganga. The Vientiane Declaration on Mekong and Ganga initiative had called for efforts to advance new linkages in knowledge-based sectors as well as in old economy areas like transport corridors and infrastructure development. The linkages between India and these countries will give New Delhi an opportunity to speed up economic development of its North-East region and this is exactly what the North-East region of India need.

Table 4.5: Composition of Informal Imports under India-Myanmar Border

Commodities	Percetage Share in Total Value		
	Moreh Sector	Champahi Sector	Overall
Textile and foot wear	11.87	29.43	17.39
Blankets	4.16	10.17	6.76
Food and beverages	10.47	6.44	9.24
Livestock		25.75	5.15
Electrical items	57.38	16.74	43.25
Plastics and sybthestic items	6.52	2.23	5.26
Utensils	3.81	2.19	3.49
Cosmetics	2.9	1.67	2.65
Consumer goods	9.11	5.49	6.74
Precious stones		0.34	0.07
Total	100.00	100.00	100.00

Source: 1. National Informatics Centre and NEDFi, <neidatebank@hub.nic.in

2. Reserve Bank of India, Guwahati for 2003-04

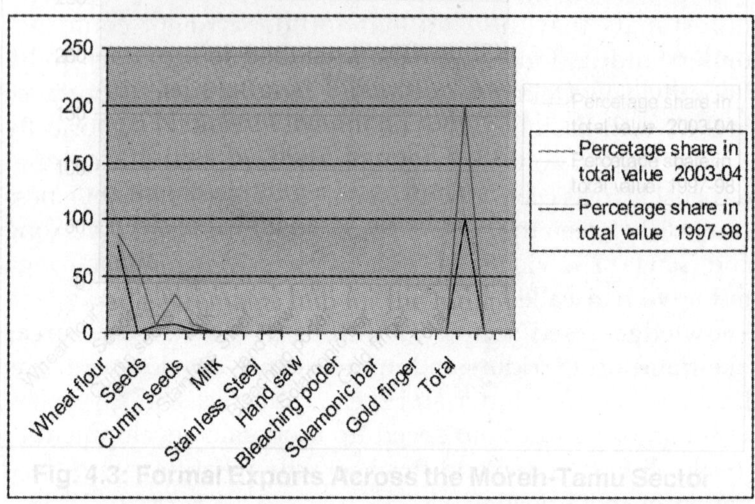

Fig. 4.3: Formal Exports Across the Moreh-Tamu Sector

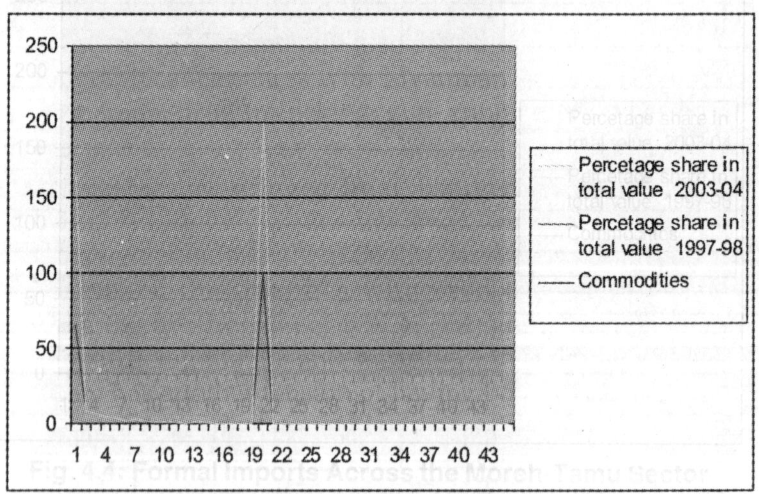

Fig. 4.4: Formal Imports Across the Moreh-Tamu Sector

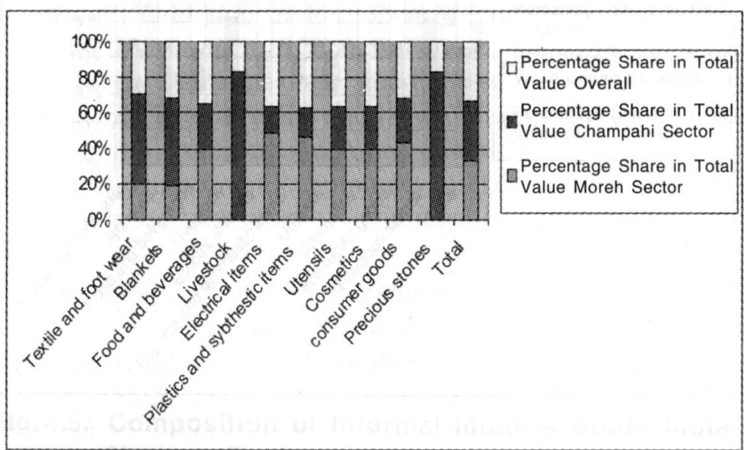

Fig. 4.5: Composition of Informal Imports Under India-Myanmar Border

Peace and Good Governance: Keys to Development

When debate are going on for more economic integration of North-East India with the economies of ASEAN countries, apprehensions have also appeared from various angles which urge the policy makers to direct their policies more vigorously for bringing peace and good governance in the states of the region. Peace and good governance are the two basic keys for development which the region lacks for a considerable level (Verghese, 1996). While from one side separatist and extremist activities are restricting the investors from out side the region, lack of good governance with its contribution to ever growing corruption is making the investors to think twice before investing in the region. It is highly important to have a just law and order and a governance system to get maximum benefits from economic activities.

All the eight states in the North-East region are affected by the ethno- cultural and economic- political extremists' movements from long time. Assam which is regarded as the most prosperous state within the region is the ground for insurgent groups like United Liberation Front of Assam

(ULFA), Karbi Liberation Organization (KLO), National democratic Front of Bodoland (NDFB), Dima Halong Deoga (DHD), Adivasi National Liberation Association (ANLA), Karbi-Longri Natioanl Liberation Front (KLNLF) etc. Regular terrorist activities by these banned outfits through bomb-blasts, and thereby killing a large number of innocent people at different places of the state posed as a threat to peace and development.

Bangadesh remains hub for the Indian Insurgent groups. Illegal migration from Bangladesh in Assam which has become a national security issue, provided ground for jihadi forces to build up strong network in the state. It, even, has created apprehension in the mind of the native people of a possible take-over by Bangladesh.The movements by the way of protests, demonstrations, bandhs by various organizations have also led to the breach of peace.

Arunachal Pradesh, although, is not much affected by insurgency, has bases of NSCN and ULFA in certain areas. It is also affected with the problem of migration from Bangladesh which has posed a threat to the social and economic life the hill tribes residing there.

Disturbing elements are also found in Manipur. Due to its geographical closeness with Myanmar, border crimes like narcotic trade, drug trafficking, gun- running are reported in regular basis.

Nagaland has suffered from insurgency for last several decades. Though cease fire has been announced between Government of India and NSCN (IM), and working for almost fifteen years, the state has witnessed the group clashes between the two fraction of NSCN (IM) and NSCN (K). This has jeopardizing the life and security of the common people. The state has another tension of having border disputes with Assam and also with states of Manipur and Arunachal Pradesh due to the demand of greater Nagaland in NSCN (IM), compromising parts of the states of Assam, Manipur and Arunachal Pradesh (Vashum, 2000).

Rest of the states in the region is also not free of conflict. Ethnic conflicts, growing unemployment, easy money making culture through illegal means are common to these states.

When the question of development comes it automatically brings in need for good governance as a permanent necessity. The rate of corruption in the North-East region is also considerably very high. Growing corruption in the public offices has not only created income imbalances, but also has fueled extremist activism in the region. Due to corruption in the public field, resources have not properly been utilized and resulted in a slow rate of development (Hussain, 2004).

In order to bring prosperity and development in the region, steps have to be taken for maintenance of peace and establishment a fare system of governance. Once peace comes, investment will follow, and then development process will start, and the people will feel integrated with the rest of the country. Too long North-East has felt isolated, neglected, and cut off from the mainstream. "Look-East" policy where North-East is regarded as a gateway ASEAN has once again made this region a focus of attention for all the right reasons.

5

Conclusion

Ever since the beginning of structural adjustment process in India economy in the early 90s', a new orientation is sought to be given to India's foreign policy with a thrust on Southeast Asian countries. This shift in country's foreign policy under the concrete shape of Look-East policy has provided scope not only for economic integration but also for more political engagement having security dimension with the ASEAN countries. For a relationship that began about a decade ago with recognition of India as a sectoral dialogue partner of ASEAN in 1992. Mutual interest led ASEAN to invite India to become a full dialogue partner of ASEAN during the fifth ASEAN summit in Bangkok in 1995 and a member of the ASEAN Regional Forum (ARF) in 1996. India and ASEAN have also been holding summit level meetings on an annual basis since 2002.

Besides, India has also been involved in a continuous effort to upgrade the bilateral relationships with the ASEAN member countries. For example, India has entered into an agreement with Thailand for a free trade area (FTA). This was followed with a similar agreement with Singapore in a Comprehensive Economic Cooperation Agreement (CECA). Sub-regional cooperation has accelerated too. The Mekong-Ganga Cooperation (MGC) and the BIMST-EC (Bangladesh,

India, Myanmar, Sri Lanka, and Thailand Economic Cooperation) are indicators to this effect.

India's initiative in proposing an FTA with ASEAN signifies its desire to develop close economic linkages. Although this proposal was made five years before it still has not become a reality due to India' s negative list factor. In this context, India's policy makers have to proceed with long term beneficial strategy. It is significant that the items in the negative list have been considerably reduced in March 2007. The ASEAN is also somehow not relenting on some of the issues.

The setting up of an India-ASEAN Regional Trade and Investment Area as a long-term objective should be the main focus of India-ASEAN relationship. Both must enter into broad-based bilateral agreements in areas such as science and technology, IT, space technology application, financial services, human resource development, cultural engagement, education etc. Tenuous issues could be handled separately.

India's participation in the first-ever East Asia Summit in Kuala Lumpur in 2006 marked a new high in India's 'Look East policy'. It provided ground for India to go one step ahead of its inclusion in the Asia Pacific Economic Cooperation (APEC). These developments are having positive political and strategic impact. While India is trying for more integration with ASEAN counties, East Asians countries particularly China sees India's engagement as a proactive diplomacy towards Southeast Asia which mat threaten its growing influence. India through her "Look-East policy" is seen by some analysts to balance China. India wants cordial relationship with China as it is essential from India's point of view if it is to be part of emerging East Asia Community.

Ever since the mid-1990s, every study of North-East region talked of the need to pursue the "Look-East policy". The close proximity of North-East in terms of border and culture with ASEAN region is a accepted fact whose potential had to be tapped and used for India's diplomatic success in Southeast Asia. This study has pointed that North-East region can emerge as a prospective linkage between India and ASEAN, provided the policy makers utilize the existing prospects with proper policy directives and sensitivity.

The concept of developing North-East as gateway to ASEAN is the result of India's Look-East policy which was formulated in the 1992, as a vision of late Prime Minister P.V. Narashimha Rao. North-East India shares 1643 km long boundary with Myanmar that passes through the states of Arunachal Pradesh, Manipur, Mizoram and Nagaland. In this sense it carries a geo-political importance. Its strategic location vis-à-vis the ASEAN region has become significant and made Indian foreign policy makers to take congruence of seeing the usefulness of building North-East India as a bridge between India and Southeast Asia.

Though the region had become land-locked as a result of India's partition, it was a gateway to the East and Southeast Asia before independence through the historical Silk Road. The paradigm shift in Indian economy and parallel shift in the foreign policy direction made the policy makers search for the old border connectivity for greater engagement with booming economies of the ASEAN countries. Naturally North-East India due to its geographical closeness has become important in the Look-East policy framework. Moreover, development took place only in the recent past. In the first decade since the declaration of the Look-East policy, not much notice was taken of the North-East.

Traditional connectivity of the region, in terms of culture and ethnicity, with the Southeast Asian countries is a significant factor. The people of Tai origin found in the North-Eastern region are also inhabitants of ASEAN countries like Thailand, Combodia and Laos. People having their origin in Myanmar are also found in the states like Manipur and Nagaland. These people not only share common cultural and ritual but having also much lingual commonality. Cultural diplomacy is an important factor of soft power which India is learnt to emphasize only recently with positive response from ASEAN members.

Lack of infrastructure in the region has stood in the way of converting North-East India into gateway to Southeast Asia. From the part of the Ministry of Development of North-Eastern Region (DoNER) to the Union Ministry of Industry and commerce number of positive steps have been taken for proper infrastructure development in the region. Trade liberalization with Myanmar through Moreh-Tamu sector and Champhai and the decision to open up historic Stilwell Road are considered as major developments in the whole process. The government decision to develop the Kaladan Multi-transport project will provide easier and cost effective transport opportunities for trade. While the Kaladan project will provide access to most of the ASEAN countries, the Stilwell Road will go one step ahead by connecting Kunming in China. In this sense North-East India can emerge as an Export Processing Zone (EPZ). The travel distance between Ledo to Kunming, the connecting points of Stilwell Road in India and China respectively, is almost equal to that of New Delhi and Ledo. The Asian Highway project is another potential bridge between India and Southeast Asia. Air connectivity among the North-East region and the ASEAN countries is required and with the Guwahati-Bangkok flight was a welcome step in the right direction. It is very unfortunate that this flight only due to commercial reason could not continue. Government should introduce even more direct flights connecting others parts of Southeast Asia from LGB international airport Guwahati. ASEAN countries too should extend their visa offices to Guwahati from Kolkata for greater track II diplomacy, trade and commerce.

Despite proposed plans to have improved infrastructure for border trade, there has not been any major initiative for the improvement of intra-state connectivity in the North-East region. The states in the region have extremely poor transport infrastructure. Except for Assam no other state in the region has direct air connectivity with the rest of India which means they are left isolated. For promotion of exports and trade, the region first needs intra-state trade among themselves.

Self-sufficiency would enable them to strengthen their economic base. Improved intra-state transport infrastructure is essential for promoting tourism which is one of the crucial areas of bonding India with ASEAN. For tourism to succeed effective flood control measures need to be taken as North-East region is a major flood porn area. According to Sanjoy Hazarika, "Since the main road and rail corridor of the region is under water or is affected by water for long period every year, without substantial investment in water transportation the Look-East policy will run in to the sandbanks of the Brahmaputra".

Thus economic, political, traditional and cultural factors have contributed towards the process of placing North-East India as a major component of Look-East policy. To give effect to this process a large number of administrative measures need to be taken. The recommendations of various studies to develop infrastructure at Moreh and open up other trade points has also seen considerable progress. So far "Look-East policy" has not brought any concrete economic gains to the North-East Region. To look at the long-term effect of the "Look-East policy" for the North-Eastern states, it is important to understand some important principles governing import, export and overall trade.

As for geographically contiguous areas the most common form of trade is border trade, it is appropriate that "Look-East policy" first try for more trade relation between North-East region and Myanmar. Though the process was started a decade ago with the formalization of agriculture trade under the Indo-Myanmar Trade Agreement, due to lack of institutional format, a larger portion of border trade is still informal. The government should try for a just exchange rate between Indian rupee and Myanmar's kyat to have more formalized border trade. The government has to keep in mind that for further trade with China and other ASEAN countries by land route, all movements have to be through Myanmar. Myanmar's strategic location can not be ignored. There is a limit to trade promotion strategy via the North-East region as trade promotion via West Bengal and maritime route of Bay of Bengal is more cost effective. A transport subsidy given to North-East states is unlikely to overcome this problem. In fact, troubled relations in Manipur has made even the relatively more developed Moreh trading post relatively redundant, to the extent that informal trade will need greater incentives to convert to legal trade and formal trade is unlikely to divert via Manipur in place of West Bengal.

Formal arrangements for trade via North-East region to the ASEAN countries have more or less been decided, but many question whether the North-East region is itself ready for that? The region is not economically as developed as many of the other states in India. As said by Sanjib Baruah , "North-East India's isolation from its neighbourhood has much older roots: that which came about as a result of the advent of western domination over sea route and over global trade and more particularly the British conquest of the region and decisions to draw lines between the hills and the plains, to put barriers of trade between Bhutan and Assam and to treat Myanmar as strategic frontier- British India's rulers built a major transport infrastructure, aimed primarily at taking tea and other resources out of Assam, disruption of old trade routes remained colonialism's most enduring negative legacy." One cannot help asking will reopening of trade routes through North-East India lead to economic development of the region? Although we do not have a uniform answer to this question, one thing is common to all the academic studies and that is that local industrial productions need to be improved along with agriculture. Entire infrastructure will have to be revamped and hotels, restaurants, resorts will have to be built for the international tourists.

An attempt is being made to identify the export potentials which are within the range. Though agriculture is the main occupation for majority of people in all the states, except Tripura and Manipur, agriculture is not doing well in other states. However potentials are high in agriculture because of the favourable climate, land and labour inputs. Export possibilities are high in plantation corps. Assam produces almost half of India's and 15 per cent of world's tea. Properly blended and carefully produced Assam tea will be able to increase tea export to the presently non-traditional markets. Assam can also convert some of its area to green tea as green tea market is quite extensive in East Asia. North-East region also produces good quality of fruits like pineapples, Pears, bananas, oranges and vegetables like chillies, ginger, pumpkins, cucumber, tomatoes etc. With proper storage and packaging these items can be exported to the neighbouring markets. Considering agricultural as a vital item of border trade the North-East Vision 2020 document (2007) states as following:

> *"Promoting trade between the NER states and the neighbouring countries then requires going beyond the calculations of 'geographical contiguity' and looking at those commodities in which the NER states have a comparative advantage in an economic sense. Here two main points need to be made. First, there are a few agricultural items in which the NER states have a comparative advantage vis-à-vis the rest of the country (see chapter 1 on Agriculture). The NER states can actively consider trading these items only when their own domestic surpluses become sufficient, and domestic surpluses are constrained by the lack of marketing due to uncoordinated production efforts of the individual states. This is particularly true in the case of fruits and vegetables. Second, it is debatable that NER trade with neighbouring countries is always more profitable (and hence more likely) than with the mainland. Many growth centres like Kolkata, Delhi and Mumbai offer economically larger markets than those of Bangladesh and Myanmar. This is already showing up in the nascent floriculture industries of the NER where exports are mainly to Guwahati, Kolkata and Delhi and even to Holland at the international level. Third, the dynamics of trade in agricultural products is somewhat different from the dynamics of trade in industrial goods. Trade in agricultural items is generally of the inter industry variety since product differentiation is not easy while trade in industrial goods admits*

of so-called 'intra-industry" trade. In agricultural items the excess demand in the NER states for items like meat, meat products and fish make them potentially important import items, so supplies from neighbouring states are likely to be cost-effective. However, this is largely ruled out by the restrictions on such trade, for example, in the Indo-Myanmar trade agreement. Further, the trade pattern of Indo-Myanmar and Indo-Bangladesh trade indicates that the demand of both Myanmar and Bangladesh is largely for industrial items such as processed foods and drinks (including animal foods), miscellaneous mineral and manufactured goods, textile fibers, textiles and clothing, and machinery and transport equipment. The NER states are unlikely to generate any production capacity for export in the relevant items in the near future (see the chapter on Industry). While there is a good possibility for exports of agro-processing industries and floriculture-based industries, it is debatable that the best markets for these lie in the adjoining countries. Hence, the immediate need seems to be to promote trade in basic agricultural commodities (rice, fish, pulses, etc.)."(NE Vision 2020, 2007)

North-East India also has favourable climate for rubber plantation. A good beginning has been made under high yielding varieties of rubber in Assam and Tripura. In fact Tripura has been declared as the second rubber capital of India by the Indian Rubber Board. So steps are to be taken for the enlargement of its export possibilities. In addition, North-East is rich in medical plants. Arunachal Pradesh is reported to have more than 500 species of medical plants. In Manipur the investment requirement on medical plants has been estimated at Rs. 100 to Rs. 132 crores. Nagaland also has variety of medical plants. The available plants in the region include agar, tejpatta, dalcheni, mints etc. Assam too has vast forest reserve having medical plats with investment potentials. Steps have to be taken for collaboration of these units with India's export oriented pharmaceutical industry.

The ASEAN markets have already shown an interest for some of the industrial products of North-East India. Products manufactured from plantation crops such as jute, mesta, and ramie have proved their popularity in the Asian market. Assam is one of the leading producers of good quality jute in the world and enjoys a competitive advantage along with vast potential in cane and bamboo products. Considerable work has been done in this industry and it has been exhibited in various national and international exhibitions. Another area of great potentiality is handlooms and handicraft. Assam silk and particularly muga which is known as golden silk can get substantial place in the neibouring markets.

Despite the above mentioned prospects, various analysts have expressed apprehensions in the ongoing process. The major apprehension is to the national security. Myanmar being used by the major terrorist outfits of the North-East India for camps and shelter. This is serious concern. The slow approach to opening up of the major trade route connecting Myanmar through North-East India is also due to the above mentioned threats. Though these trade routes will give economic advantage to the region, these could be used for easy access to illegal arms supply to the terrorists groups in the region. Besides, these groups may also get access to free cross border movement. China which has been showing its hegemonic role in the North-Eastern part of India since the 1962 war may create some security problems in future. China already has good diplomatic relationship with Myanmar and may use its soil for destabilizing India's North-East. In the late 80s and early 90s due to the growing bases of terrorists groups in Myanmar India cut of its diplomatic relations with Myanmar's military junta. This vacuum was filled up by China with its support to the authoritarian military regime in Myanmar. India soon realized that isolating Myanmar will lead to adverse effect in terms of peace and stability in its North-East region and started engaging with Myanmar. India like ASEAN adopted a policy of constructive engagement vis-à-vis Myanmar. The sub regional grouping like BIMSTEC and MGC were initiated to strengthen economic and diplomatic linkages with Myanmar.

Opening up of trade routes may also pose possible jihadi threat in the North-East region of India, particularly in the state of Assam which is already facing the illegal migration problem from Bangladesh. It is a known fact that some fundamentalist groups in Southeast Asia are networking with international Islamist jihadi movement. There is a possibility of its expansion to the North-East India through the border roads.

Another cross border issue which is of equal serious concern is the issue of drug trafficking and HIV/AIDS. Since Myanmar is the second largest producer of opium in the world after Afghanistan, it may in near future see North-East India as effective market. There is a possibility of expansion of 'golden triangle', world famous for narcotic smuggling, to the North-Eastern region of India.

Drug trafficking across the common border of Myanmar and the three states of Manipur, Mizuram and Nagaland has gone up to a serious level. Myanmar itself supplies 20 million rupees of drugs to the North-East region per month. The drug mafias to enter into the north-east India through More sector in Manipur and Champhai in Mizuram. Most dangerous impact of this drug trade is that the students' community has become involved with it. New trade routes and transport infrastructure will give more easy access to the drug traders. Many addicts use intravenous injections to push drugs and contact HIV Aids. North-East India ranks second in HIV porn areas in the country. Importance of dialogue partnership has helped India facilitate a joint task force with the ASEAN countries to fight drug trafficking.

To conclude that in spite of its short coming the "Look-East policy", is a welcome step. But things are to be properly directed so that maximum benefit can be provided to the local people in the region. Though after the liberalization of Indian economy the country has witnessed almost 9 per cent GDP growth, regional disparity in terms of income is a harsh reality and India's North-East region is clear example of it. The economic integration of the region with the ASEAN countries will definitely bring prosperity and development to the region.

References

(*indicates primary sources)

Books

Acharya, Amitabh (2000), *The Quest for Identity: International Relation of South East Asia*. Singapore: Oxford University Press.

Agrawal, M.M (1996), *Ethnicity, Culture, and Nationalism in North-east India*. New Delhi: Indus Pub. Co.

Ambatkar, Sanjay (2002), *India and ASEAN in the 21st Century: Economic Linkages*. New Delhi: Anmol Publications.

Ayoob, M (1990), *India and Southeast Asia: Indian Perceptions and Policies*. London and New York: Routledge.

Bandopadhaya, P.K (2007), *THE North-East Saga*. New Delhi: Publication Division, Min. of I & B.

Banerjee, Dipankar (1997), *Myanmar and North East India*. New Delhi: Delhi Policy Group.

Barua, Alokesh (2005), *India's North-East Developmental Issues in Historical Perspective*. New Delhi: Manohar Publication.

Barua, B., and N.N Deodhai Phukan (1964), *Ahom Lexicons*. Guwahati: Department of Historical and Antiquarian Studies in Assam.

Baruah, Sanjib (2004), *Between South and Southeast Asia: Northeast India and Look East Policy* (Ceniseas Paper 4). Guwahati: Centre for Northeast India, South and Southeast Asia Studies.

Baruah, Sanjib (2005), *Durable Disorder: Understanding the Politics of North-East India*. New Delhi: Oxford University Press.

Baruah, Sanjib.(1990), *India Against itself: Assam and the Politics of Nationality*. New Delhi: Oxford University Press.

Bhaumik, Subir(1996), *Insurgent Cross Fire: North-east India. New Delhi*: Lancer Publishers.

Das, Gurudas and R.K. Purkayastha (eds.) (2000), *Border Trade: North-east India and Neighbouring Countries*. New Delhi: Akansha Publishing House.

Das, Gurudas. et al. (2005), *India-Myanmar Border: Status, Problems and Potentials. New Delhi:* Akansha Publishing House.

Devare, Sudhir (2006), *India and Southeast Asia: Towards Security Convergence*. Contributor Institute of Southeast Asian Studies: Institute of Southeast Asian Studies.

Dixit, J.N (2001), *Indian Foreign Policy and its Neighbours*. New Delhi: Gyan Pub. House.

Egreteau, Renaud (2003), *Wooing the Generals: India's New Burma Policy*. New Delhi: Author Press, Centre De Sciences Humaines.

Ghosal, Baladas (ed.) (1998), *ASEAN and South Asia: A Development Experience*. New Delhi: Sterling Publishers.

Ghosh, Subir. (2001), *Frontier Travails – North-East: The Politics of a Mess*. New Delhi: Macmillan.

Gogoi , Kiron Kumar (2004), *Historiology of Mongoloid People*. North-East India: Ban-Ok Pup- Lik- Myung- Tai.

Gogoi, Padmeswar (1968), *The Tai and the Tai Kingdom; With a Fuller Treatment of the Tai-Ahom Kingdom in the Brahmaputra Valley*. Guwahati: Department Publication, Gauhati University.

Gopalakrishnan, R (1990), *Ideolog, Autonomy and Integration in the North-East India: (Issues in Political Geography)*. Guwahati: Omsons Publications.

Gopalakrishnan, R. (1991), *North-East India: Land, Economy and Peoples*. Delhi: Har Anand Publications.

Gordon, Sandy and Stephen Henningham (eds.) (1995) *India Looks East: An Emerging Power and its Asia Pacific Neighbours*. Canberra, Australia: Strategic and Defence Studies, Australian National University.

Grare, Frederic and Amitabh Mattoo (eds.) (2001), *India and ASEAN: the Politics of India's Look East Policy*. New Delhi: Manohar Publications.

Guha, Amalendu (1977), *Planter Raj to Swaraj*. New Delhi: People Publishing House.

Hazarika, J (1996), *Geopolitics of North-East India*. New Delhi: Gyan Publication.

Hazarika, Sanjoy (2000), *Rites of Passage: Border Crossings, Imagined Homelands, India's East and Bangladesh*. Delhi: Penguin Books.

Hazarika, Sanjoy. (1995) *Strangers of the Mist: Tales of War and Peace from India's North-east*. New Delhi: Penguin Books.

Kumar, Mahendra (1967), *Theoretical Aspects of International Politics*. New Delhi: Shiva Lal Agarwal & Company.

Kumar, Nagesh (ed.) (2004), *Towards an Asian Economic Community: Vision of a New Asia*. New Delhi. RIS for Developing Countries and Singapore: Institute of Southeast Asian Studies

Kumar Nagesh, Sen Rahul, Asher Mukul (2006), *India-ASEAN Economic Relation: Meeting the Challenges of Globalization*. New Delhi: RIS for Developing Countries and Singapore: Institute of Southeast Asian Studies.

Lintner, Bertil (1996), *Land of Jade: A Journey from India Through Northern Burma to China*. Bangkok: White Orchid Press.

Ludden, David. (2004) *Where is Assam? Using Geographical History to Locate Current Social Realities.* Guwahati: Centre for Northeast India, South and Southeast Asia Studies.

Misra, Udayon. (2000), *The Periphery Strikes Back: Challenges to the Nation-state in Assam and Nagaland.* Shimla: Indian Institute of Advanced Study.

Murayama, Mayumi, Kyoko Inoue and Sanjoy Hazarika (2005), *Sub-regional Relations in the Eastern South Asia: With Special Focus on India's North Eastern Region.* Tokyo: Institute of Developing Economies.

Nag, Sajal. (2002) *Contesting Marginality: Ethnicity, Insurgency and Subnationalism in North-east India.* New Delhi: Manohar.

Nanda, Prakash (2004), *Rediscovering Asia: Evolution of India's Look East Policy.* New Delhi: Lancer Publisher.

North-East India (2002) *a Bibliography.* New Delhi: Nehru Memorial Museum and Library.

Prakash Shri, Vanita Roy and Sanjay Ambedkar (eds.) (1996), *India and ASEAN: Economic Partnership in the 1990s and Future Prospects.* New Delhi: Gyan Publishing House.

Ray, Jayant Kumar and Prabir De (eds.) (2004), *Promotion Trade and Investment in Eastern South Asia Sub-region.* New Delhi: Bookwell.

Ray, Syamal Kumar (2003), *India's North-east and the Travails of Tripura.* Kolkata: Minerva Publications for Maulana Abul Kalam Azad Institute of Asian Studies.

Reddy, K. Raja (ed.) (2005), *India and ASEAN: Foreign Policy Dimensions for the Twenty First Century.* New Delhi: New Century.

Sachdeva, Gulshan.(2000), *Economy of the North-east: Policy, Present Conditions and Future Possibilities.* Delhi: Konark Publishers.

Sarker, Himansu. Bhusan (1985), *Cultural Relation Between India and Southeast Asian Country.* New Delhi: India Council for Cultural Relation.

Sarma, Atul and Pradeep Kumar Mehta (2002), *Exploring Indo-ASEAN Economic Partnership in a Globalising World.* New Delhi: Bookwell.

Sharma, Manorama (1998), *History and History Writing in North East India.* New Delhi: Regency Publications.

Shastri, Ajay Mitra (2002), *Ancient North-East India.* New Delhi: Aryan Books International.

Sridharan, Kripa. (1996), *The ASEAN Region in India's Foreign Policy.* Aldershot: Dartmouth Publishing Company.

Srivastava S C (1987), *Demographic Profile of North East India.* Delhi: Mittal Publication.

Subba, T.B. and G.C. Ghosh (2003), *The Anthropology of North-east India.* New Delhi: Orient Longman.

Terwiel, B.L (1980) *The Tai of Assam and Ancient Tai Ritual.* Gaya: Institute of South East Asian Studies.

Vashum, R. (2000), *Naga's Right to Self Determination: Anthropological-historical Perspectives.* New Delhi: Mittal Publications.

Verghese, B.G. (1996), *India's North-East Resurgent: Ethnicity, Insurgency, Governance, and Development.* New Delhi: Konark Publishers.

Verghese, B.G. (2001), *Reorienting India: the New Geo-politics of Asia.* New Delhi: Konark Publishers.

Articles

Acharya, Amitav (2003), "Southeast Asia. Imagining the Region". *Himal South Asian.* 16 (1).

Ambatkar, Sanjay (2001), "India ASEAN: Emerging Scenario in Economic Interaction", *India Quarterly*, 57(1): 99-120.

Ambatkar, Sanjay (2002), "Evaluation of India ASEAN Economic Cooperation Since 1985", *Regional Studies*, 20(4): 72-97.

Akoijam, A. Bimol and T. Tarunkumar (2005) "Armed Forces (Special Powers) Act 1958: Disguised War and its Subversions". *Eastern Quarterly* 3(1) 23-30.

Asher, Sen, Srivastava (2003), "ASEAN- India: Emerging Opportunities" in *Beyond the Rhethoric, The Economics of India's Look East Policy*. New Delhi: Manohar Publication.

Barbora, Sanjay (2002), "Ethnic Politics and Land use: Genesis of Conflicts in India's North-East", *Economic and Political Weekly*, 37(13):1285-95.

Barbora, Sanjay (2002), "Ethnic Politics and Land Use: Genesis of Conflicts in India's North-East". *Economic and Political Weekly*, 37(13): 3756-60.

Barua, Alokesh and Bandyopadhyày. A (2005), "Structural Change, Economic Growth and Regional Disparity in North-East: Regional and National Perspective" in *India's North-East Developmental Issues in Historical Perspective*. New Delhi, Manohar Publication.

Barua, Indira (1977), "The Ahoms; An Appraisal of Reviving and Revitalizing Trend" in *Cultural and Biological Adaptabilities of Man with Social Reference to the North-Eastern Region*. Dibrugarh: Department of Anthropology.

Baruah, Sanjib (2002), "Gulliver's Troubles: State and Militants in North-East India", *Economic and Political Weekly*, 37(41): 4178-82.

Baruah Sanjib (2005), "A New Politics of Race: India and its North-east", *IIC Quarterly*, 32 (2&3): 165-76.

Batayal, A. (2004), "ASEAN's Quest for Security: A Theoretical Explanation". *International Studies*, 41(4): 48-53.

Bezbaruah, M.P (2001), "Tourism in the North-East India", *Dialouge* 2 (4) 49-55.

Bezbaruah, M.P (2007), "Agricultural Development in the North-East: Status, Sssessment and Prospect", *Indian Journal of Agricultural Economics*, 62(1): 52-56.

Bhadra, R K (2002), "Administrative Responses to the Identity Problems and Social Tensions of the Tribal Communities in North-East India", *Indian Journal of Public Administration*, 48(3): 390-99.

Bhattacharya, Swapan K (2006) "India's Economic Relations with the ASEAN Countries: Competitiveness, Complementarities and Strategies for Future Growth", *World Focus,* 27(4): 28-32.

Bhattacharya. P (1996), "Status and Potentiality of Tourism in Assam", Paper Presented in NEIGS Annual Conference.

Das, Parimal Kumar (1997), "India Moves Towards ASEAN", *World Focus,* 18(6): 10-12.

Dasgupta, Anindita (2001), "Small Arms Proliferation in India's North-east: A Case Study of Assam". *Economic and Political Weekly,* 36(1): 3646-52.

Dasgupta, J.(1997),"Community, Authenticity and Autonomy: Insurgency and Institutional Development in India's North-east". *The Journal of Asian Studies,* 56(2).

Datta, Sreeradha (2000), "Security of India's North-East: External Linkages", *Strategic Analysis,* 24(8): 1495-1516.

Devi, T.Nirmala (2004), "Emerging Trends of Economic Cooperation, the India-ASEAN". *Journal of Contemporary Asia & Europe,* 1(1):116-33.

Fernandes, Walter (1999), "Conflict in North-east: A Historical Perspective", *Economic and Political Weekly,* 34(51): 3579-82.

Gaur, Seema (2003), "Framework Agreement on Comprehensive Economic Co-operation Between India and ASEAN: First Step Towards Economic Integration", *Asean Economic Bulletin,* 20(3): 283-91.

Ghosal, Baladas (1997) "ASEAN Identity". *World Focus,* 18(6): 7-9.

Ghose, Sanjoy (1997), "Civil Society in North-East", *Mainstream,* 35(26):33-35.

Gohain, Hiren (1997), "Ethnic Unrest in the North-East", *Economic and Political Weekly,* 32 (8): 389-91.

Goswami, Homeswar and Gogoi Jayanta Kumar (2005), "Trading Across China, Myanmar, Bangladesh and India: Impact on North-East India" in Alokesh Barua (eds) *India's North-East developmental Issues in Historical Perspective.* New Delhi, Manohar Publication.

Hazra, Jayati (2002), "Health and Development of North-East India" *Geographical Review of India*, 64(1): 21-32.

Hixley, T. (1987), *ASEAN's Prospective Security Role: Moving Beyond India-China Fixation*. 'Contemporary Southeast Asia' 9(3): December.

Hong, Zhao (2007), "India and China: Rivals or Partners in South-East Asia", *Contemporary Southeast Asia*, 29(1): 121-42.

Hussain, Monirul (2004), "Food Security and the North-East", *Economic & Political Weekly*, 39(41): 4515-16.

Hussain, Monirul (2004), "Governance in the North-East", *Dialogue*, 5(4): 45-170.

Jha, Ganga Nath (1997) "ASEAN and India: Dawing of New Partnership". *Indonesian Quarterly*, 25(2): 152-66.

Jha, Pankaj (2005), "BIMST-EC: A New Regional Initiative", South Asia Politics, 4 (1): 49-51.

Kamboj, Anil (2006), "Conflicts in North East India: An Overview", *World.Focus*, 27(11): 19-25.

Kappen, Thomas Risse (1991), "Public Opinion, Domestic Structure, and Foreign Policy in Liberal Democracies", *World Politics*, 43 (4), pp. 479-512.

Kashyap, Abhaya (2006), "Look-east' Policy", *South Asia Politics*, 5 (9): 21-26.

Kaul, M.M (2006), "An Overview of BIMSTEC and MGC". *South Asian Survey* 13(2): 313-322.

Khanna, V (2000), *'India and East Asia: Huge Synergies to Tap'*, Business Times, 5 May.

Kotwal, Dinesh (2000), "Instability Parameter of North-Eastern India", *Strategic Analysis* 24(1): 137-149.

Kuri, Pravat Kumar (2003) "Factor Market Imperfections and Explanations of Tenancy: Testing of an Econometric Model Using Evidence from Assam of North-East India", *Indian Journal of Agricultural Economics*, 58(2): 234-45.

Lall, Marie (2006), "Indo-Myanmar Relations in the Era of Pipeline Diplomacy". *Contemporary Southeast Asia*, 28(3): 424-446.

Lim, R (1998), "The ASEAN Regional Cooperation: Building on Sand". *Contemporary Southeast Asia* 20(2).

Madhab, Jayanta (2000), "Agriculture: Key to Development of North-East", *Dialogue,* 2(2): 49-61.

Maharana, Dilip Kumar (2007), "India-ASEAN Relations in the 21st Century: Areas of Cooperation and its Prospects", *South Asia Politics,* 6 (6): 30-37.

Malik, M. (1994), "Sino-Indian Rivalry in Myanmar: Implications for Regional Security". *Contemporary Southeast Asia* 16(2).

Mishra, Deepak K (2007), "Gender, Forests and Livelihoods: A Note on the Political Economy of Transition in North-east India", *Social Change,* 37 (4): 65-90.

Muni, S. (1997), "India and South-East Asia: Challenges and Opportunities". *Contemporary Southeast Asia,* 19(2).

Murthy, Gautam (2004) "Revitalizing India-ASEAN ties", *Journal of Contemporary Asia & Europe,* 1(1): 111-15.

Naidu , G V C (1996), "India and ASEAN" Strategic Analysis, 19(1): 65-72.

Naidu, G.V.C (1999), "ASEAN: Challenges Ahead and Implications for India", *Strategic Analysis,* 23(2): 283-97.

Nath, Dev (2005), "Hill Economies of the North-eastern Region: Emerging Challenges and Opportunities", *Economic & Political Weekly,* 40(25): 2486-91.

Neogi, Debasis (2007), "Ensuring Rural Development in North-East India: Need for Intensified Extension, Technology Transfer and Industrialization", *Political Economy Journal of India,* 16(1-2): 1-9.

Oinam, Anand. (2003), *Look East Policy and Manipur.* 'The Sangai Express' (Imphal, Manipur): 27 December.

Ojendal, J. (2004), "Regionalism in South-East Asia Under Unilateral Pressure". *International Organization,* 80(3).

Parthasarthy, G (2008), "Opportunities and Challenges", *Seminar.* No. 584, 39-42.

Pillai, S K (2001), "Human Factor in the Economy of the North-East", *Dialogue,* 3(2): 93-106.

Prabhakara, M.S. (2004), "Is North-East India Landlocked?" *Economic and Political Weekly'* 39(42): 4338-42.

Pramanik, Bimal (2006), "Demographic Shifts in Bangladesh and its Impact in the East and North-East India" *World Focus,* 31(4): 3-7.

Puri, Harish K (1998), "Fifty Years of India's Independence and the North-East", *Mainstream,* 36(11): 13-19.

Rao, P.V (2006), "4th India-ASEAN International Summit on India and New Asia", Journal of Indian Ocean Studies, 14(3): 467-68.

Robb, Peter. (1997), "The Colonial State and Constructions of Indian Identity: An Example on the North-east Frontier in the 1880s". *Modern Asian Studies,* 31(2): 36-40.

Roy Burman B K (2001) "For Overcoming the Schizophrenic Alienation of the North-East: Outline of a Comprehensive Approach", *Mainstream,* 39(45): 13-19.

Roy Burman B K (2005), "Grey Areas in Demography of North-East India", Mainstream, 42(34): 18-22.

Roy, Sanjay K (2005), "Conflicting Nations in North-East India", *Weekly Economic & Political,* 40(21): 2176-82.

Sachdeva, Gulshan (2005) "North- Eastern Economy: New Policy Options" in Alokesh Barua (eds) *India's North-East Developmental Issues in Historical Perspective.* New Delhi, Manohar Publication.

Sahani, V. (2004), "From Security in Asia to Asian Security". *International Studies,* 41(3): 56-60.

Satish Chandra India (2000), "The ASEAN and the Indian Ocean", *Journal of Indian Ocean Studies,* 7(2-3): 107-15.

Scott, David (2007), "Strategic Imperatives of India as an Emerging Player in Pacific Asia", *International Studies,* 44(2): 123-40.

Sundararaman , Shankari (2007), "India-ASEAN Relations: Search for Opportunities in a Shifting Regional Scenario", *World Focus*, 28(11): 425-30.

Selth, Andrew. (1996), "Burma and the Strategic Competition Between India and China". *Journal of Strategic Studies*, 19(2): 25-29.

Sen, Rahul, Mukul Asher and Ramkishen S. Rajan. (2004), "ASEAN-India Economic Relations: Current Status and Future Prospects". *Economic and Political Weekly* 39(29): 3823-27.

S. Shimray, Ungshungmi (2001), "Ethnicity and Socio-political Assertion". *Economic and Political Weekly*, 36(39): 3247-51.

Sharma, B.D (2007), "Aspects of Education in the North-East", *Dialogue*, 8(4): 89-115.

Shimray, Ungshungmi. (2004), "Socio-political Unrest in the Region Called North-east India". *Economic and Political Weekly*, 39(42).

Singh, Udai Bhanu (1999), "India and the ARF: The Post-Pokhraan II Phase" *Strategic Analysis*, 22(10): 1591-1606.

Singh, Udai Bhanu (1999), "Outlook for the ARF: Relevance for India", *Strategic Analysis*, 23(6): 965-90.

Singh, Udai Bhanu (2006), "Geo-economic and Geo-strategic Importance of Myanmar in India's 'Look East Policy" in *Engagement and Development: India's North-East and Neighbouring Countries*. New Delhi: Akansha Publication.

Sridharan, Kripa (2004), "Wooing the Generals: India's New Burma Policy". *Contemporary South-East Asia*, 26(2).

Srikanth, H (2005), "Discourses on Rights and India's North-East", *Economic & Political Weekly*, 40(4): 335-36.

Suryanarayan, V (1999), "Indo-Asean matrix", *Journal of Indian Ocean Studies*, 6(3): 234-45.

Shri Prakash (2004), "India-China-ASEAN" *World Focus*, 25(9):19-20.

Taher, M (1993), "The Peopling of Assam and Contemporary Social Structure", in *Social Structure and Regional Development*. Raipur: Rawat Publication.

Terwiel, B.J (1983), "Ahoms and Study of Early Tai Society", *Journal of the Siam Society* 71: 42-62.

Umdor, S (2007), "Economic Infrastructure in North-East India: An Analysis", *Man & Development*, 29(1): 113-30.

Verghese, B.G. (2004), *Borders Matter more than Boundaries from the North-east Looking Out*. 'Man and Society: A Journal of North East Studies' 1(1): Spring.

Yahya, F. (2003), "India and South-East Asia Revisited". *Contemporary South-East Asia* 25(1): 342-48

The Hindu.

Internet Sources

The Asian Highway.URL: http// www.e-peo.net

* Department of Commerce, Government of India (2006) *"India's Trade with East Asia and the ASEAN"*,URL: http// www.commerce.nic.in

Lectures/seminars/conferences (2007), *"India- ASEAN Vision 2020"* sponsored by Minister of Development of North Eastern Region (DoNER), URL: http//www.ris.org/lecture_prabirde.html

*Indian Embassy China (2004).

URL: http//www.indianembassy.org/policy/foreign_policy/2004/2004

*Minister of Development of North Eastern Region (DoNER) (2006), "Pursue Open Sky Policy for Air Lings to BIMSTEC and ASEAN Country",

URL: http//www.mdoner.gov.in/dfmain1.asp?

*Ministry of External Affairs (2007) *"ASEAN-India Relations"*, URL: http//www.nea.gov.in

*Ministry of SSI & DoNER(2003), *"Development of Cane and Bamboo Industry in NE Region"*,URL: http// www.planningcommission.nic.in/news

NEDFi (2006).URL: http//www.neidatabank@hub.nic.in

*North Eastern Region Vision 2020

URL: http//mdoner.gov.in/writereaddata/newsimages/final6963338914.pdf

*Press Release (2007) by DoNER, URL: http//www.pibaizwal.nic.in

*Prime Minister's Speech (2005), "Fund to DoNER for Early Completion of India-ASEAN Free Trade Agreement", URL: http//www.pindia.nic.in/speech.asp

M.P. Bezbaruah (2005) "Prospects for Tourism". URL: http// www.india-seminar.com/2005/550/550%20m.p.%20bezbaruah.htm

The Kaladan Project

URL:economictimes.indiatimes.com/India_Myanmar_quietly_finalise_Kaladan_project/articleshow/

The Kaladan Project.

URL:economictimes.indiatimes.com./India_Myanmar_quietly_finalise_Kaladan_project/articleshow/

The Ledo Road. URL: http//www.geocities.com/nicchg/stilwell.html

The Stilwell Road.URL:http// tinsukia.nic.in/subpages/stilwell.html

Trans-Asian highway mooted to boost economy of northeast (2007)

URL: http//www.sinlung.com/print/886html

*UN ESCAP (2004), Asian Highway.

URL: http//www.unescap.org/jecf/p06highway.htm

*ASEAN Secretariat (1995), URL: http// www.aseansec.org/5187.htm

*ASEAN Secretariat (2003), URL: http//www.aseansec.org/ar04.htm

The Assam Tribune, *23rd November, 2004*, www.assamtribune.co.in

The Assam Tribune, *17th April, 2007*, www.assamtribune.co.in

The Assam Tribune, *12th Feb, 2008*, www.assamtribune.co.in

Index